No Other Way

No Other Way

LaSalle R. Vaughn

 Unless otherwise identified, Scripture quotations are from the New International Version of the Bible.

Take note that the name satan and related names are not capitalized. We choose not to acknowledge him, even to the point of violating grammatical rules.

Treasure House
an Imprint of
Destiny Image
P.O. Box 310
Shippensburg, PA 17257

"For where your treasure is
there will your heart be also." Matthew 6:21

ISBN 1-56043-765-0

For Worldwide Distribution
Printed in the U.S.A.

Destiny Image books are available through these fine distributors outside the United States:

Christian Growth, Inc.
Jalan Kilang-Timor, Singapore 0315

Lifestream
Nottingham, England

Rhema Ministries Trading
Randburg, South Africa

Salvation Book Centre
Petaling, Jaya, Malaysia

Successful Christian Living
Capetown, Rep. of South Africa

Vision Resources
Ponsonby, Auckland, New Zealand

WA Buchanan Company
Geebung, Queensland, Australia

Word Alive
Niverville, Manitoba, Canada

Contents

Chapter 1

God's Plan for the Family

The devil has targeted the family.

If you don't believe that the devil has the family as his chief concern right now, just take a look around at what's happening in your immediate family, in families throughout your neighborhood, and throughout this country. Marriages are falling apart.

Wives get phone calls from husbands who don't even come home. Their husbands just call up and say, "I've had it." They may have been married for thirty years, but the husband—or wife—will say, "I'm throwing in the towel. I'm tired of it." People who have been married almost a lifetime are finding themselves suddenly single.

Then some of them try to make themselves available to see if they can find another mate. And the children are looking on. And they're concluding that there's no hope for this thing called the family.

Our answer must be to follow God's plan. Only His plan for the family will work. Only by following God's plan will our marriages, our families, be able to withstand all the attacks of the devil.

To discover God's plan for the family, we'll look to the Bible. We need our plans grounded in the Word of God if we want our families to be reflections of His will. Unless we are holding ourselves to a biblical standard, we won't know where we're supposed to be going, or how we're going to get there. And we won't even recognize it when we're under attack by the devil.

Some Christians don't even realize what's happening. We can watch television and learn that the Clinton administration is giving special support to homosexuals. We see that the government is supporting sex education in school, and forbidding courses that recommend that teens abstain from sex. They call abstinence a religion because it says that human reproduction is different from, higher than, animal reproduction. We can see Madonna's pornographic book on the best-seller list. Some Christians can see all this and not realize that it's an attack against the family as an institution, and also against their own particular families.

As far back as the Eisenhower administration, in the 1950's, people were trying to redefine the family, to make two homosexuals a legally married couple and allow them to adopt children. They didn't succeed during Eisenhower's time, but they seem to be succeeding today. Some of the radical elements in society are saying—hoping—that in the next decade the family as we know it will cease to exist. Biblical values, they believe, are holding up progress, preventing the establishment of a new world order. And they're right. Our families are a bulwark against the tide of evil.

We must stand for family values, because family values are God's values. The family is important to God. God established the family, and His Church is a family, and the Bible tells us that marriages are supposed to be patterned on the relationship of Christ and His Church.

To achieve that pattern, we will have to look at the values we live by, not just in marriage, but in dating and in how we prepare for marriage. Some people think that Christians shouldn't date at all. I have no problem with Christians dating, but there need to be some guidelines.

We need to prepare for marriage according to God's plan, and choose our mates according to His plan. Problems in a marriage affect the family. You can't get away from it. When a husband and a wife are not of one accord, it's going to affect the children. And most of those problems come from people being selfish in their marriages.

Often they're inclined to be selfish because they can get out of marriages so easily now. If people don't like the way their spouse is acting, they can claim that they're no longer compatible. And what happens? The children suffer. When husbands and wives become selfish, they stop caring about the children. All they care about is their personal happiness—and it's worldly happiness they're seeking, not happiness according to God's plan.

If we want happiness, we must obey the commands God has given the husband and wife. Whether we like it or not, we must obey.

Obedience is the way to happiness for children too. Nowadays we sometimes hear children talking to their parents the way their parents talk to them. When I was growing up, I was afraid to even think about disobeying. I could not imagine a child telling a parent, "I'm not going to do it." Now kids will say, "If you hit me, I'm going to call 911 on you." Some kids are doing that right now.

Such problems, such rebelliousness and selfishness, come from the parents, from problems in the marriage.

There are three major problems in marriage, I think. One is sex. The second is money. The third is communication. Those three problems seem to predominate.

To overcome these problems, we will look for biblical answers. Let's begin with Genesis 2, beginning at verse 4.

> *This is the account of the heavens and the earth when they were created.*
>
> *When the Lord God made the earth and the heavens —and no shrub of the field had yet appeared on the earth, and no plant of the field had yet sprung*

up, for the Lord God had not sent rain on the earth, and there was no man to work the ground, but streams came up from the earth and watered the whole surface of the ground—the Lord God formed the man from the dust of the ground and breathed into his nostrils the breath of life, and the man became a living being.

Now the Lord God had planted a garden in the east, in Eden; and there He put the man He had formed. And the Lord God made all kinds of trees grow out of the ground—trees that were pleasing to the eye and good for food. In the middle of the garden were the tree of life and the tree of the knowledge of good and evil.

A river watering the garden flowed from Eden; from there it was separated into four headwaters. The name of the first is the Pishon; it winds through the entire land of Havilah, where there is gold. (The gold of that land is good; aromatic resin and onyx are also there.) The name of the second river is the Gihon; it winds through the entire land of Cush. The name of the third river is the Tigris; it runs along the east side of Asshur. And the fourth river is the Euphrates.

The Lord God took the man and put him in the Garden of Eden to work it and take care of it. And the Lord God commanded the man, "You are free to eat from any tree in the garden; but you must not eat from the tree of the knowledge of good and evil, for when you eat of it you will surely die."

The Lord God said, "It is not good for the man to be alone. I will make a helper suitable for him."

Now the Lord God had formed out of the ground all the beasts of the field and all the birds of the air. He brought them to the man to see what he would name them; and whatever the man called each living creature, that was its name. So the man gave names to all the livestock, the birds of the air and all the beasts of the field.

But for Adam no suitable helper was found. So the Lord God caused the man to fall into a deep sleep; and while he was sleeping, He took one of the man's ribs and closed up the place with flesh. Then the Lord God made a woman from the rib He had taken out of the man, and He brought her to the man.

The man said, "This is now bone of my bones and flesh of my flesh; she shall be called 'woman,' for she was taken out of man" (Gen. 2:4-23).

This was the first marriage ever, the first family. Scripturally speaking, a man and a woman can be considered a family.

For this reason a man will leave his father and mother and be united to his wife, and they will become one flesh.

The man and his wife were naked, and they felt no shame (Gen. 2:24-25).

Later, in Genesis 4, we read:

Adam lay with his wife Eve, and she became pregnant and gave birth to Cain. She said, "With the help of the Lord, I have brought forth a man." Later she gave birth to his brother Abel (Gen. 4:1-2).

What do we see here? A man plus a woman is a family. A man plus a woman and a child or children is a family. Or a single parent with a child or with children may make up a family.

Here we have the biblical pattern. Now, in the eyes of God, a man and a man do not make a family. A woman and a woman cohabitating do not make a family.

But in our country today they're trying to redefine the family, to change the family from what the biblical pattern, the Word of God, calls for.

I'm talking about family in the sense of cohabitating, having sex, and having children. I almost threw up one night when my wife called me and said, "Honey, you've got to come see this." And there were two men who had adopted two boys, and the men were saying they would spend time together, go to PTA meetings and everything, and that they would be just as much a family as anyone else, and they didn't want anyone to discriminate against them.

People like these are having a larger and larger impact on our society. Do you know what's going to happen eventually? They're going to try to affect the Church sooner or later. They not only want these aberrant lifestyles accepted, they want the biblical standard of family done away with.

Now, God intended for man and woman to multiply. If two men get "married," they can't multiply. That "marriage" or "family" cannot be in God's purpose. It is completely against God's Word. Two women do not have the seed to plant and multiply either.

In the normal course of things, in God's plan, a family will include offspring. That's the way God intended it. And there's no other way. No other pattern can substitute for God's pattern of the family.

In First Corinthians 11 we see the world's way contrasted with God's way. Those who believe in the Bible, in the Word of God, strive to live their lives according to what God's Word has to say, whether they like it or not. In the end, things always prove that God is right anyway. AIDS is an example—it's a natural consequence of sin, a sign that God was right all along about homosexuality. But even if AIDS had never come about, homosexuality would still be wrong. God said so. AIDS is just one natural example that proves Him right.

We have to live according to God's Word. He knows what's right and what's best for us. We don't know what's going to happen down the road. He does.

Now let's look at First Corinthians 11:3. God created lines of authority and everything will function smoothly because of it. Lines of authority have been established in business, government and family. *"Now I want you to realize that the head of every man is Christ, and the head of the woman is man, and the head of Christ is God."*

The head of Christ is God, God the Father. That is the God-ordained order of the family. Headship doesn't mean that the man is supposed to be smarter than or better than the woman. It doesn't mean that at all. It means that in God's perspective, the man is supposed to be the head of the woman.

God the Father is the head of Christ. They are equal. But the Bible tells us that Christ did not deem equality with God something to be grasped at. The family is supposed to reflect that. The woman is the equal of the man, but Christlike living means that equality is not something to be grasped at.

And the children are not the equals of the parents. Some people worship their children. The children run the household. You'll hear them say, "Dad, I ain't going to church. And you can't make me either." That's backwards. That's putting children at the head and Christ at the bottom. But the divine order is just the reverse.

And what is the result of putting things in reverse order? We've lost respect for the family. We've lost respect for authority in the family. We've lost discipline. The Bible says, "Spare the rod and spoil the child." Some people disregard that Scripture and say, "I'm not spanking them. It just hurts me too much."

My father used to tell me all the time, "It hurts me more than it's gonna hurt you." As children we didn't believe that, but as parents we find out that it does hurt us to spank our children. And some of us neglect our duty because we find it painful. That's not taking up our cross. That's not following Christ. That's following our own desire to do only what we feel comfortable with. We're not supposed to live by our feelings but by the Word of God.

Parents can abuse their authority by the way they treat their children, maybe telling them ten times, "Go downstairs and get me a glass of water." Parents can act like they're sitting on the throne. We might spank the children for something they didn't do, and never tell them, "I'm sorry." It takes a real man or a real woman to say, "Look, I was wrong. Can you forgive me?" When we do that, it strengthens the credibility of the authority.

You need to strengthen your authority as a parent, because children learn how to manipulate their parents. The children won't take no for an answer. They get on your nerves. They wear you down. Just to get rid of them, you say, "Just go ahead. Get out of my hair."

Children are all natural lawyers too. They find the loophole. Let me tell you how my daughter Elisha does me. She says, "Dad, do you have any money?"

"No, Elisha, I don't have any money."

"Okay," she'll say, "I guess you don't mind if I take some of this change off this dresser up here, right?"

I'll say, "There's no change up there." When I come home I usually dump all my change on top of the dresser.

When I tell her not to take any of my money, she thinks I'm telling her not to go into my wallet. But she takes all of my change. My daughter is never without money because she feels I've given her the green light to do this.

One woman in our church recalled how she used to manipulate her mother. "When she would come home, I would have the whole house cleaned when I wanted something, or wanted to do something."

"Some children bring up their parent's actions, even if it was in the past," another man told me. The kids bring up some negative things to justify what they want to do.

Another way children manipulate their parents is to compare what other children have and what they don't have.

A serious and dangerous form of manipulation occurs when teenagers threaten their parents by saying, "If you don't let me, I'll move out." Or they'll threaten to run away, or worse, to kill themselves.

Another problem is that husbands and wives sometimes undermine each other's authority. Tammy goes to her daddy and says, "Daddy, let me use the car."

Daddy says, "I'm not going to let you use the car."

So Tammy goes to her mom and says, "Mom, Dad's not going to let me use the car."

Mom says, "Go back and tell your daddy that I said to let you use that car or else." The authority and headship of the house is being weakened, because the child is manipulating the parents.

Tammy goes back and says, "Dad, Mom said you had better let me use that car or else."

That comment attacks the father's manhood. So he's going to say, "You tell your mama that you will get this car over my dead body."

Now you have the parents against one another and the authority has gone from that house. The man has been dethroned, emasculated, and the woman has lost her position, too.

The opposite of that is in God's plan, what we read about in Genesis: unity; the two shall become one. Too often there's no unity in the family any more. What's causing that? Career decisions, for one thing. We have both husband and wife working, and maybe pursuing a career is more important to them than the unity of the family. When they're both so devoted to their careers, there can be a lack of communication, because the family no longer puts value on sitting down and talking and sharing with one another, which is very important.

Dinner is a good time for fellowship. Sometimes, though, the children are so busy, they want to go do their own thing, and they aren't interested in these family moments. Sometimes, but not always, it's a sign of rebelliousness. But sometimes the wife cooks dinner at home, and the children don't have the common decency to tell her that they're not going to be home for dinner. When this happens, it's time for a family meeting.

How many of us still have family meetings? How many have never had a family meeting? Be honest. A good time to have family meetings is when you need to go out of town. When my wife and I have to travel, we bring all the kids together for a meeting. We tell them, "When we're gone, we don't want this or that to be going on. Don't forget to put the trash out. Don't forget to take care of this. Check the mail. Put the lawnmower in at night. What are some of the things you're going to be doing next week?" You can't just let things go haywire.

You have to have order. A man is the pastor of his home. Some of us think we're called to be pastors of churches. First, we have to pastor the sheep God has given us: our wives and our children. That's your congregation. Your wife is your co-pastor. Your children are your members.

We need to have order. A family should have clear goals. A lot of families are not making any kind of progress because they don't have any goals. They need to have some "*we goals*." "*We goals*" are family goals. They state, "This is what '*we're going to do*' as a family." Then you can talk about "*I goals*," *individual goals*. Once we have our "*we goals*" established, we can help each other with our individual "*I goals*"; going to school, getting a job or buying a car, etc.

A lot of families don't care enough to establish goals, or to work together to meet the family or individual goals. The husbands and wives only care about themselves, about being happy. There's more at stake. There's more to life than your happiness.

This focus on individual happiness has contributed to the loss of respect for men in this country. Many women are disappointed in men, because society leads them to expect so much. And it kills the men on the inside, particularly black men. We need women to help us to be men. We're asking you to let us be men. There's nothing worse than a manipulated man. There's nothing worse than a woman who can manipulate a man to get him to do anything that she wants. When a woman manipulates a man so much that he can't think for himself, he will never reach the full potential God has planned for him. He will never be the man that God has called him to be.

As a pastor, I've talked to four different men who were impotent, and one reason they were impotent was that their wives were dominating them. We live in a masculine oriented society that says to be feminine or submissive is equatted with weakness. This is a lie from the pit of hell. Society has caused the woman to leave her family to seek employment to assist her husband. Competition has been placed between men and women in the workplace. Consequently, a lot of relationships today are almost like two people of the same sex (men) living together. They both come home tired and they lose the intimacy they used to have because they both are competing for the masculine role in the home. It's difficult for a man to respond sexually to someone acting just like him.

Men must be careful never to dominate women either—to dominate a woman to the point where she can't be her own person and celebrate her uniqueness is a definite turn off for her. God never intended men to dominate women. Domination can be a form of control and manipulation. Domination, control and manipulation will hinder your wife from becoming the person God intended her to be. There needs to be a balance there. That means putting our family values ahead of our own desires and our own egos. Otherwise we're bringing trouble to our families. Proverbs 11:29 says: *"He who brings trouble on his family will inherit only wind, and the fool will be servant to the wise."*

Never ignore your family. Help the family meet its goals and needs. In First Timothy 5:3-6 we read:

> *Give proper recognition to those widows who are really in need. But if a widow has children or grandchildren, these should learn first of all to put their religion into practice by caring for their own family and so repaying their parents and grandparents, for this is pleasing to God. The widow who is really in need and left all alone puts her hope in God, and continues night and day to pray and to ask God for help. But the widow who lives for pleasure is dead even while she lives (1 Tim. 5:3-6).*

This principle applies not just to widows. We are obligated to look after the needs of our families. If we let our own desires and our own egos get in the way of meeting our families' needs, living only for pleasure, the Bible calls that being dead even while we're alive.

If a person is part of the Church, and they have no one else in the world, the Church has a responsibility to take care of them. But Scripture says that if they have children or grandchildren, those family members should be taking care of them.

We always have a responsibility to our families. When a member of the family has a crises in their life, we have a responsibility to help them. But in our society today we get wrapped up in our own little worlds, and we feel like we don't have any responsibility toward our mother and father when they get old. The Word of God says we have a responsibility to them. We have a responsibility to help our parents when they grow old. We have a responsibility to help our spouse grow into the person God wants him or her to be. We have a responsibility to guide our children into mature Christian adulthood.

It is essential that we exercise our responsibility, because the devil has targeted the family. He is out to destroy it. He is out to destroy *your* family. We won't overcome his attacks unless we model our families according to the Word of God and live up to the responsibilities God has given us.

We have to stop living according to our own selfish priorities, and start putting our lives in order according to God's priorities.

Reflections

1. Only God's plan for the family will work.

2. To discover God's plan for the family, look to the Bible.

3. We must stand for family values because family values are God's values.

4. Problems in a marriage affect the family.

5. When a husband and a wife are not in one accord, it is going to affect their children.

6. When husbands and wives become selfish, they stop caring about their children.

7. If we want happiness, we must obey the commands God has given the husband and wife.

8. We have to live according to God's word. He know what's right and what's best for us.

9. No other pattern can substitute for God's pattern for the family.

10. Dinner is a good time for family fellowship.

Chapter 2

God's Priorities

If the devil is concerned about the family, it must be important to God. The family is so important to Him that it was the first institution that God established, by giving Eve to Adam. Today we are in need of having the family, and family values, reinstituted. We need to go back to some of the old things we used to do.

Families in America are in turmoil right now. We can bring order back into the family by reinstituting values in the area of dating, and the reasons people get married. Men and women need to regard marriage as an institution and not just a relationship. More people are getting into marriage, out of marriage and doing it more than once because many regard marriage as only a relationship and not as an institution. When we no longer find the relationship satisfying, we get out of it and use the past relationship problems as tools to make our next relationship last longer. Marriage is the highest form of relationship. It is an institution ordained by God and intended to be a permanent relationship. Many who get married over and over again are becoming relationship therapists with no regard for marriage as an institution. A lot of people have lost sight of the value of commitment. People make a commitment for one or two years, and it's almost understood that they're only going to stay married for two or three years. They expect to find someone else after they are married. And we have been throwing away our values in the name of happiness. There's no such thing as morals in the eyes of the world right now; each person is left to find his or her own formula for happiness, and that is rarely defined in terms of commitment, sacrifice and dying to self.

The world's priority is personal happiness. But we won't be happy if we let the world teach us our values. The Word of God is the only thing that must guide our values.

You can see just how bankrupt the world's values are if you look at the way the world treats people who don't go along with the crowd. You're supposed to find your own path to happiness, but if the crowd doesn't like what you're doing, they try to make you feel as if you're not worth anything.

If you're trying to follow the world's formula for hapiness, then you have to reevaluate who you are and what you stand for. If the crowd makes you feel like you're a nobody because you're a virgin, and your response is to go out and prove to them that you *can* have sex outside of marriage, you'll end up ruining your life because you want to please the crowd. God wants us to stand above the crowd.

The world says that if you're not happy in your marriage, then you're free to get a divorce. Has that made people happy? Look at how broken relationships and divorces have affected families. The result is rebellious children, dysfunctional families, children who go to school and have their minds so full of the junk that goes on at home that they can't concentrate on their schoolwork. Mommy and Daddy fuss all night long, or Mama is not talking to Daddy, or Daddy went away for two days.

The Word of God says that no one must break apart what God has joined together. The Bible teaches us that keeping a covenant is more important than personal happiness. We can enter heaven because God kept His covenant with us, even when we broke it. When we were unlovable and unfaithful, when we were wrong, He kept His covenant and saved us. Marriage is a covenant. It's meant to be kept, for better or worse.

So many people are breaking their covenants because they are not in line with God's priorities. Their priority is personal happiness. God's priority is keeping covenants, even when it meant He had to die on a cross. Even when they don't get divorced, a lot of parents are teaching their children that personal individual happiness is more important than their marriage, and many of these people really don't know how their relationship is affecting their children, because there is no communication line open between the child and the parents.

If the mother and father say, "You do as I say, not as I do. You just do it because I said it," then children don't see the value in what the parents are saying because the parents won't do it themselves. The parents will say, "I live this way because I'm grown. You don't smoke, because I tell you not to, but I can smoke. I'm an adult." It can't be such good advice if the parents won't follow it. The parents are not giving the right example to their children.

There needs to be some control coming from the parents, but it has to be coupled with example. Your kids may not do everything you tell them, but I guarantee you that they will imitate what they see. You can see what you're teaching your children by the way they behave. Are you teaching them to put God's priorities above individual happiness?

The Bible teaches that when a man and a woman get married there is supposed to be a committed relationship between them. It's a covenant with each other and with God, and of course they also make a public commitment to the church and the community when they make their vows. But they promise to stay married to each other and to no one else; they are completely dedicated to each other, completely committed to each other as companions for the rest of their lives. There should not be a third party coming in.

God hates adultery. God hates divorce. God hates sex outside of marriage. Anyone who believes in these things and willfully does these things is going against God. That's plain and simple. If God hates these things, and you believe in these things and do these things, then you are going against God.

Well, is there any gray area in the Word of God? If you're a Christian, and you've been taught the Word of God, and yet if divorce is the first thing that comes to your mind when there are problems in your marriage, and you know that God hates divorce, then you need to get some godly counsel. If you're thinking about divorce, you need to think, "I'm going against God."

The Word of God is clear. It says that you will know the truth and the truth will make you free. But sometimes the truth hurts.

When Jesus spoke against divorce, some of His apostles told Him that if they couldn't get divorced, it would be better to remain single.

Is it better to remain single? Or to put the question another way: Is living for God harder for a single person or for a married person? You might be married to a man who doesn't want you to come to church. If you're married to an unsaved person, or a person who wants all of your time, living for God can seem very difficult. But being single has its difficulties too. Is it harder to be single when your flesh cries out?

So which is better for a Christian: to be married or single? That's not a fair question, is it? But it's worth asking, because it has to do with why we get married in the first place. When the apostles' ideas bumped up against the living Word of God, some of them decided that marriage was too hard. So is it better to remain single?

I asked that question of my congregation, and these are some of the answers I got:

"If one of the spouses is doing nothing in church, and the other is very active, one might be pulling this way, and one pulling the other."

"I'm a single parent; before I was single, I was married and a Christian, but my husband wasn't. And it was hard being married in that situation, but I don't know what it is like with a Christian husband. But as a single person, I think it's easier because there's no one to get mad at. And not only that; the single person has Jesus, you know. And when you walk in the Spirit, that flesh doesn't cry out as much as when you're walking in the flesh."

What if both persons are in the Lord? Well, it should be no problem. They should be of one accord, doing the same thing and enjoying it. That can happen, and you're a blessing to each other when it does.

"I'm single, and if I have a problem with something, if I'm slipping, that's with me and God. There's nobody else there to help, to try to tell me, 'You need to get right with Him.' "

"The circumstances are different between a single and a married person. When you're single, you don't really have anyone else to answer to. You know you have mainly to concern yourself with your salvation. When you're married, you still have different challenges. It depends on the spiritual level that the couple is at."

So let's ask a question and get an answer where the rubber meets the road:

You're single; your flesh cries out; you want someone to snuggle up to at night, and the Bible tells you that sex outside marriage is wrong. The only thing you can do is grab your pillow, squeeze that pillow and say, "Lord, where's my husband?" or, "Lord, where's the wife I've asked You for? When are You going to send someone into my life?" And you see married couples walking around. They have someone to hold and snuggle close to, right? Is that easier for a single person to deal with than the problems you face when you're married and you're supposed to be one, but you're not?

Here are some of the answers I got:

"No, it's not easier, but it depends on what spiritual level you're at. I was single, so I know."

"My prayer was that I asked God to take that feeling away from me, because I didn't need it being single."

Now, why should God take that feeling away from you?

"Well, He gave it to you. The desire for a mate comes from Him. But as a single person, I don't need to have it. Why be tormented? So, you pray and ask God to take it away, so you don't have to be tormented."

"For months at a time I didn't have to worry about that. But now, being married, I've got another person to be concerned about all the time. There's a constant thing there. Whether it's good or bad, it's always there, even if you're going through it with the Lord."

"One of the greatest battles for single men or women is the flesh, whether it be sex, whether it be loneliness, whether it just be an intense battle."

"You connect singles with sexual conflicts. That is an issue. I admit that. But that's not the only issue. Ecclesiastes 4:9 (KJV) says this: 'Two are better than one; because they have a good reward for their labour. For if they fall, the one will lift up his fellow, but woe to him that is alone when he falleth; for he hath not another to help him up.' When you're married, there's two people to share and to make the decisions, and when you're single, it's only you. And when you're single, you only have to think about those things of God, and when you're married, you have each other to think about, so you can't totally concentrate on the things of God."

"A single person has God. Someone who's married has God. And if you're raised in two separate churches, even though you both believe in God, you may have different beliefs in God, and you may understand the Bible differently than each other, so it's just as hard. You still have God to follow."

Single women and men need to make a commitment to wholeness before they enter into a relationship and especially marriage.

Commitments in marriage can distract a person from his or her commitment to God. For some, it is better not to get their lives so involved. Look at First Corinthians 7:7-9. For some people, it's better to stay single. Paul said:

> *I wish that all men were as I am. But each man has his own gift from God; one has this gift, another has that. Now to the unmarried and the widows I say: It is a good for them to stay unmarried, as I am. But if they cannot control themselves, they should marry, for it is better to marry than to burn with passion* (1 Cor. 7:7-9).

Remaining single offers more time with the Lord, in a sense, doesn't it? But Paul was saying, "If you don't have this gift to stay single, then maybe it's better that you get married." He was talking about celibacy.

Now look at First Corinthians 7:29,31b-35:

> *What I mean, brothers, is that the time is short. From now on those who have wives should live as if they had none...For this world in its present form is passing away. I would like you to be free from concern. An unmarried man is concerned about the Lord's affairs—how he can please the Lord. But a married man is concerned about the affairs of this world—how he can please his wife—and his interests are divided. An unmarried woman or virgin is concerned about the Lord's affairs: Her aim is to be devoted to the Lord in both body and spirit. But a married*

woman is concerned about the affairs of this world—how she can please her husband. I am saying this for your own good, not to restrict you, but that you may live in a right way in undivided devotion to the Lord (1 Cor. 7:29,31b-35).

A lot of men and women are more concerned about how to please their mate than they are about how to please God. There are probably a lot of men and women who would like to do much more for God. But they have to keep peace in the home.

They start coming to church a lot, and the husband or wife will start saying, "You know, you're always there. You don't ever give me any time."

Or one will be tithing faithfully and the other will say, "You're more committed to the pastor than you are to me." That person's interests are divided. A divided interest will contribute to bringing about ineffective communication, and will eventually drive the husband and wife apart.

It's important that we understand that our spouse has this kind of pull on us, or we can blindly just concern ourselves with pleasing our spouse all the time.

The same thing can happen to single people, though. They can be concerned about being deprived, concerned about what they don't have. They can be focusing on the married people, and wishing they were married. They could be the perfect one for God to use, but they can't be used, because they're preoccupied with their own desires. They're being told to focus on that desire. You go into a restaurant and you'll find two chairs at every table; it tells us that people are not supposed to be alone. And that if you're not married, something's wrong with you. Even in the church, which is probably the ideal situation, we're breeding the world's idea that if you're not married, if you're not having this wonderful kind of relationship, you're missing out on something. So it's even infiltrating the church.

But let me tell you something: when this culture of ours dictates how we're supposed to act, then we have problems. We must point to the Word of God. Among the Corinthians there were single people who had the same feelings that single people have right now. God knows what we're facing. As we said, He made us, and He gave us the desire for a mate. But that has to be secondary, because we have a higher priority: union with Him. We can choose marriage or the single life, as long as it's consistent with drawing closer to Him.

But we can't start letting the world tell us how we're supposed to be, because then we will let the world control us, and not let ourselves be controlled by the Word of God.

I was in the Air Force, and my wife and I were often separated. Some women, even to this day, are waiting for their husbands to come back from Vietnam. They don't have the assurance that their husbands are dead, and they're still waiting. And in that situation, or in situations less extreme, when you let the world speak to your mind, you'll be tempted to throw commitment out the window. When you look around and you see that you're going to be living like a single for two years, waiting for your husband or wife to come back, you start saying, "I have needs." "I'm not having my needs fulfilled." And even though we're married, we start thinking that we can't wait for him or her to come back. The world says that you don't have to wait, it is more important to have your needs fulfilled.

But this doesn't just apply to careers like the military. For any couple, there may come a time when you are separated. We must understand that marriage is more than just being happy. Marriage calls for commitment and dedication.

God Almighty still sees a man and a woman coming into marriage as virgins. Regardless of whether you come as a virgin or not, regardless of what the world is saying, this is what God sees. This is old-fashioned, isn't it? God has designed a woman's body to reflect a covenant relationship. When a man and woman enter that sacred act of sex on the first night of marriage, the hymen's broken, which is a shedding of blood, indicating a covenant relationship.

The world tells us that if you don't have sex outside of marriage, then when you get married, you won't have any experience. Young people don't want anyone to think they're not experienced. Don't ever think that you have to be experienced to go into a marriage relationship with someone you love, because God has designed this so that both of you can learn as you go. Remember, Adam and Eve had no prior experience. It gets better, because you communicate. As you grow together, you learn what each other likes and dislikes, and you will become experienced at pleasing each other. It will be something healthy. But if you go out and get "experience" without the lifelong commitment of marriage, you're still spiritually bonded to these people—Paul tells us that if a man has sex with a prostitute, he is united to her—spiritually and psychologically, and sometimes physically too, if you've picked up infections, you bring all these other people into bed with you when you get married.

God intends that husband and wife come to each other fresh and clean. That's what He intends. Many times it doesn't work out that way.

"Sometimes it's intimidating," one person in my congregation told me, "if a virgin, male or female, marries someone who's experienced. How do you know you're going to like what that person does if you don't have anything to compare it to? Well, if you don't have anything to compare it to, then you think you have the greatest. Then you're not missing anything."

This is serious business. It has to do with why people get married, who they marry, and when. A lot of people are marrying the wrong people. A lot of people are getting married before they should. And a lot of people are getting married too soon. They need to remain single until they become a whole person.

Many are getting married for the wrong reasons. Some people get married only for sex. Or they get married for money, or to have somebody to take care of them, or to get away from their parents. Some people get married because they had a baby or are pregnant. Sometimes people get married because they had sex, and there's a soul tie there. Some get married to acquire U.S. citizenship, or for status—married people have a certain status about them, don't they? Or they get married because they're getting old. They think they'd better go ahead and get someone before its too late. Of course, people do get married for love.

What should our reasons be for getting married? Obviously, a decision as important as marriage should line up with God's priorities, with His Word. The primary reason people marry is because they love the person. But you must understand what love is before you marry a person for love.

God loved us while we were still sinners. Love means accepting someone for who he or she is. Don't ever fall in love with someone solely on his or her potential. They may never reach their potential. And you're stuck.

I asked my congregation what love means. Here are some of their answers:

"Deep understanding, respect and loyalty."

"A willingness to go through anything with that person."

"Love is a giving experience."

Love is a continual giving experience. Love is a commitment. Love is also a decision.

Marriage is the union of two people, a man and a woman. It's a coming together of two individuals, who are now one.

A man has his own ideas. He has attitudes, and his way of doing things.

A woman has her own ideas, her attitudes, and her ways of doing things. If marriage is a union of two individuals, then what we have is a union of ideas, attitudes and ways of doing things.

We want a perfect marriage. We may not get that, but we can at least have a marriage that can work—when a man can accept and tolerate the ideas, attitudes, and ways of doing things that his wife brings to the marriage, and when the woman can tolerate and accept the ideas, attitudes, and ways of doing things that the husband brings. We have to remember that we are different. But when we get married, we bring things together. And we learn how to tolerate, and accept. The whole Christian experience, including marriage, is a continual growth process. There should always be growth in your life.

We know that we serve a holy God. And sin separates us, not just from God, but from each other. Jesus Christ unites us. He makes it possible to unite with our holy God and with each other, to grow closer to God and to each other. This is what we should be looking forward to when we get married: growth. And growth only comes when you allow the truth to free you.

This is God's priority for us, in our lives and in marriage. And we need to keep His priority in mind in living out our marriage covenant and in choosing a mate.

Reflections

1. More people are getting into the marriage and divorce cycle because many regard marriage only as a relationship, not as an institution.

2. Marriage is the highest form of relationship. It is an institution ordained by God and intended to be a permanent relationship.

3. God wants us to stand above the crowd.

4. God hates adultery. God hates divorce. God hates sex outside of marriage.

5. Single women and men need to make a commitment to wholeness before they enter into a relationship—especially marriage.

Chapter 3

Dating: Choosing a Mate in God's Will

The terms "dating," "courtship" and "engagement" have always been used to designate various degrees of commitment.

Today the term "dating" seems to carry no connotation of commitment. Today's approach to dating seems to suggest a form of recreation. It also suggests a "window-shopping" attitude, with no commitment to buy what is on display. I disagree with this. Some Christians are against dating. I personally have no problem with Christians dating other Christians. But for Christians, dating should be marriage-oriented behavior.

Singles should not be dating each other unless it is part of the process of finding a mate. Dating is serious business. Of course it can be, and ought to be, fun. You want to marry someone whose company you enjoy. But in dating you should be trying to discern the right partner to spend your life with, because marriage is a partnership, and choosing that person is probably the single most important decision you'll ever make, aside from choosing Jesus as your Savior.

Ecclesiastes 4:9-12 talks about partnership.

> *Two are better than one, because they have a good return for their work: If one falls down, his friend can help him up. But pity the man who falls and has no one to help him up! Also, if two lie down together, they will keep warm, But how can one keep warm alone? Though one may be overpowered, two can defend themselves. A cord of three strands is not quickly broken* (Eccl. 4:9-12).

That tells us about the strength of partnership: it makes us stronger. With a life partner in marriage, it's easier to resist the devil. It's easier to overcome all of the troubles that come your way. When two people are supporting each other and praying for each other, both of them should find it easier to draw nearer to God.

Dating should help you find a partner for that kind of marriage. Don't continue in a relationship if there's no possibility of marriage. You're wasting your time. Why would you involve yourself in a relationship where you have to fight off the glamour of sex, fight off the compromising, when you know you're planning on dating someone else? Never involve yourself for a period of time with someone you aren't considering marrying. If that relationship is not going anywhere, you're wasting your time.

Above all, let Christ be your guide in dating. That means that you need to set some guidelines before you even get started. There are different levels of maturity for single people in the Lord. You should always involve yourself in wholesome activities. Some people should limit themselves to group dating. Some people can't go out on a dinner date because they might do something else afterwards.

If you're mature enough to date alone, just the two of you, then stay out of each other's apartments. You should be able to say to each other, "I love the Lord Jesus Christ, and I don't want to bring any shame to Him, so if we're going to date, this has to be done in a way that will glorify Him."

Your convictions from the Holy Spirit, and what the Word of God has to say, should be guiding you. The Holy Spirit should be your invisible chaperone when you're dating. It should be like Jesus is with you. Even when other people are not around, your commitment to Jesus Christ, your commitment to His Word, can keep you where you need to be.

Give no place to the devil. Don't ever put yourself in a compromising position. Never compromise your beliefs on a date. Even with another Christian, you could find yourself saying, "It's just you and I; let's just go ahead and do this, because nobody else knows, and you won't lose any respect for me." If you're doing something that compromises your beliefs, whether it's with a baby Christian or a mature Christian, you are going against God. Single Christians must exercise discipline when dating. The heart of discipline is being able to decide in advance. The best way to prevent yourself from getting into something ungodly is to decide what your're going to do before the thing happens. Don't wait until you get into a situation where you might have sex outside of marriage to make a decision. Don't argue with your feelings. Just tell your fellings, "I've decided in advance, I'm not going to have sex before I get married." Discipline is talking back to your emotions. Discipline helps you to commit to God's Word. Deciding in advance helps you to practice self control. Self control is a choice. You make the commitment to do it before anything comes up. Anything uncontrolled in your life will weaken your life.

What about going to a person's house at two o'clock in the morning? What about taking a shower when your boyfriend's there and you're sitting there talking to him with a towel on? You shouldn't even shower when he's in the house, right?

Sexual temptations are one of the biggest problems singles have when dating. Dating can be a dress rehearsal for marriage. Dating can also be an undressing rehearsal for marriage.

Why is this such a problem? Why are so many single people and married people getting into affairs and one-night stands? Why are married and single people so fascinated with sex outside of marriage? Why are men so fascinated with having sex with someone other than their wives?

I asked my congregation this, and these are some of the answers I heard:

"Because they know there's no commitment there. It's an ego trip for a man to know that he can have other women. They think that one woman is not enough. A lot of men boast about that kind of thing. They're deceived by the lust of the flesh, trying to live out their fantasies."

"If a person has been hurt, in a marriage, if the wife finds out that her husband has had an adulterous affair, she'll go out and do it just to hurt him back."

Sometimes it's because people's needs are not being met in a marriage. And sometimes those needs are never even being communicated. Maybe they don't even know what those needs are.

There are moment-to-moment needs. A lot of men and women do not know how to meet these needs, because they don't know the needs of the other person, and we all have needs.

Until a person knows Jesus Christ, he or she will never experience the real love that God intended for a man and a woman. There are needs that your husband or your wife may not be able to meet. I have needs my wife doesn't know about—that I may not even know about. But Jesus knows about them. And sometimes only He can fulfill those needs.

Proverbs 7:18,21-22 talks about the glamor of sex, the fascination of sex, as a young man is led astray. The adulteress says to him:

> *Come, let's drink deep of love till morning; let's enjoy ourselves with love!...With persuasive words she led him astray; she seduced him with her smooth talk. All at once he followed her like an ox going to the slaughter* (Prov. 7:18,21-22).

The glamor of sex will lead to sin, even death.

We as Christians cannot allow the glamor of sex or the fascination of sex to lead us into sin. Dating a Christian, and establishing right away that your relationship must glorify God, and avoiding temptations to sin, are essential points. And after all, that's the kind of person you want to marry right? One with whom you can share a relationship that glorifies God, someone who will help you avoid sin?

You should avoid intimate acts that would lead to sex, because the Bible says sex outside of marriage is wrong. Another reason you should avoid intimate acts with anyone you date is that the love you think you're experiencing may not be the real thing. Having sex is no real test of real love. Having *no* sex is the real test of real love. You need to ask yourself, "Will he stay with me?" or, "Will she stay with me if there's no sex?" The average person in this world today who is not a believer will not necessarily stay in a relationship if there's no sex. So there are a lot of people getting married who don't have the real thing. They think they have the real thing because they're using sex as a test of real love.

After you have sex with someone you'll always have this question in your mind: What do I have to do to keep him or her? First, you were asking what you had to do to get him or her. "I'll do anything to get him." Then you end up saying, "I'll do anything to keep him." And when you do that, you open yourself up to heartbreak, emotional problems and everything else.

But if you date according to God's plan, then when sexual intimacy does come (in marriage), it will be the way God intended it to be and, it will bring about a closeness of purity, not forced, or perverted the way the world has it.

How will you know whether you're in love? How does it feel? I asked these questions of my congregation, and here are some of the answers I received, from both married and single people:

"When you come to the realization that you want to spend the rest of your life with that person and no one else no matter what."

"Being complete in a certain way."

"You start making decisions in terms of the two of you. You don't think solely of yourself. You think of that person also."

"You want to be with that person all the time. You think about that person. You can't even function. You turn into a fool."

"You're excited. You're motivated. You have a new purpose and meaning to your life."

"There's no other man. There's no other woman. There's just nobody else. This is the one. You feel a confidence."

"There's a settling. You just know, and there's no way to describe it except that you just know."

"Put some distance between yourselves to really find out. When we put that distance there, we felt, 'There must be something to this thing.' "

"He just said, 'Would you like to go for a walk?' I was ready to say yes, even before he asked. That's when I knew it was love. That's when I felt, 'For the rest of my life, this is it. I don't want anything else.' I felt the future."

"I don't think that you reach a point of being in love when you first start out. I think all of the feelings and everything you experience are those things that start the process, but I don't think you really actually fall into love until you've been together during marriage, and put up with all those things in the past, and stood all those tests and after nine or ten years you're still standing together regardless of what happens. I think that is when you really find out that you're in love."

"There's no such thing as a perfect match, a perfect mate. You're not going to automatically fall in love and stay like that for the rest of your life. Real love comes from work. The feelings will go away real quick after you get married, so the test comes after the first few years."

> *Love is patient, love is kind. It does not envy, it does not boast, it is not proud. It is not rude, it is not self-seeking, it is not easily angered, it keeps no record of wrongs. Love does not delight in evil but rejoices with the truth. It always protects, always trusts, always hopes, always perseveres. Love never fails* (1 Cor. 13:4-8).

Envy can cause big problems. Love does not envy. It does not boast. It is not proud. Think about relationships. Competition in a relationship between a man and a woman can bring death to that relationship.

Love is not self-seeking. Lust takes. Love gives.

Love is not easily angered.

People who want their way are easily angered. Every time you do something wrong, they just blow their stack. They are extremely critical all the time. Don't marry someone who's always critical, always easily angered.

Love keeps no record of wrongs. It won't say, "I remember when you did this or that."

Love does not delight in evil. It does not see others' mistakes as an opportunity to feel superior. It does not say, "Before we get married, you'd better straighten up your act now."

Love rejoices with the truth. It always protects. It always trusts. It always hopes. Love never fails.

You had better have real love when you get married. You had better be prepared to cope with problems and changes. People change when they are together for long periods of time. If small habits are going to become major irritations, you'd better know it before you decide to spend the rest of your life with a person. Your life will be under a magnifying glass to each other. That's why it's a good idea to go through six months of counseling. A long period of time will allow you to see each other very clearly. Engaged people should learn to watch what they do more than what they say—men especially need watching. Men can put together flowery words, but if they really love you, they'll show how much they care by what they do.

Your relationship must be one of caring—a deep, close friendship. There are different levels of friendship. Friendship can enter intimacy—deep, close friendships with persons of the opposite sex. If you're getting intimate, does the other person really care for you? People who get into affairs mostly enter friendships, and then they go deeper and deeper.

Maybe you don't have love; maybe you have infatuation—an immature relationship, pain, crying, hurting all the time. Immature relationships take away from you: they take away your self-image. You don't know who you are.

Mature relationships energize you, make you feel good about yourself. You get up in the morning and sing. Life is just great. "What's the problem, everybody?" you ask.

Real love is conceived when two people enter emotional intimacy—not dependency. Emotional intimacy is a strong feeling, a desire, a longing to be with the other person. This emotional intimacy should be the foundation of the relationship. It should not be sexual. You can be intimate without being sexual. To be intimate means to reveal yourself to each other, learning to listen and give of yourself to each other. It should be a mutual thing. But there are times when just one person allows himself or herself to enter emotional intimacy with another person, and the other person is not there. That's when you say one person's in love and the other person's not.

Real, mutual love is almost like music. It's a joining or connecting of the soul, because emotions are in the soul, aren't they? Emotion, mind, intellect—that's the soul, and that's what's involved when you're in love. But emotional intimacy is not sexual intimacy. Some people have sex, and never experience love. They can get almost dependent on that other person. Love is more than just a fleshly connection. That fleshly connection should come only when you are married. As you begin to love one another, moving into that close, close friendship, you move into emotional intimacy; when you get married, you will experience a sexual intimacy that only married people are supposed to have. A lot of people today go for the sexual intimacy, then work toward emotional intimacy.

That's why marriage should not be hasty.

So how do you choose this partner who will help you through life? Whom do you marry? God gives us choices. We can marry anyone we want to marry, except relationships God forbids, such as marrying close relatives, or marrying someone who has already married another. The Bible also tells us not to marry an unbeliever.

You could marry a fat person, a dumb person, an ugly person, a white person, a black person, a red person. You can marry anyone you want to marry, except for the restrictions God has spelled out. In Second Corinthians 6:14-17 we read:

> *Do not be yoked together with unbelievers. For what do righteousness and wickedness have in common? Or what fellowship can light have with darkness? What harmony is there between Christ and Belial? What does a believer have in common with an unbeliever? What agreement is there between the temple of God and idols? For we are the temple of the living God. As God has said: "I will live with them and walk among them, and I will be their God, and they will be My people." "Therefore come out from them and be separate," says the Lord. Touch no unclean thing* (2 Cor. 6:14-17).

When you are ready for marriage, you can make a choice. The first criterion is that your partner be a Christian. But there's more. Of course you should marry someone you love, someone you want to be around. Your partner should also have similar attitudes toward the important things in life. You should be able to agree on things like bringing up children and how money will be handled. The Bible asks, *"Do two walk together unless they have agreed to do so?"* (Amos 3:3)

An unbeliever will affect your walk with the Lord. It breaks my heart to see young ladies on fire for God who marry someone, and suddenly throw away their relationship with Jesus. A man who's on fire for God marries a heathen, and he throws away his walk with the Lord. We see it exemplified in the life of Solomon, described in First Kings 11:1-4

> *King Solomon, however, loved many foreign women...They were from nations about which the Lord had told the Israelites, "You must not intermarry with them, because they will surely turn your hearts after their gods"...and his wives led him astray. As Solomon grew old, his wives turned his heart after other gods, and his heart was not fully devoted to the Lord his God...* (1 Kings 11:1-4).

Now, this example is oversimplified, but let me tell you something: It takes only one man or one woman to pull you away from God. You'll start hearing, "Why do you have to go to church all the time?" or "I don't believe in tithing. They're just taking your money over there." "Bible study? You go to church on Sunday morning. What else do they want?" "Why can't you sit here and have a drink with me? What's wrong with that?" "Can't you smoke a joint with me? I'm your husband."

And the next thing you know, you don't want to hear the truth, because you have torment in your heart. If you know the truth, and you go against what God says, you'll have torment.

It's amazing how people will come to church until they get married. And all of a sudden the spirituality leaves them.

You may be a musician in the church, and you have to come to practice on Tuesday night, or something, and that's important to you. And this person might say, "Well, you know what? The first thing I want you to do is get out of that choir, because it's too much time." Those things that are important to you, you need to have an understanding with that person before you say, "Let's tie the knot."

Singles today who are actually living for the Lord have one of the greatest opportunities for marriage, because they can marry whom they want. They don't have to be pressured. They can wait for the best choice.

Singles in church have an excellent opportunity to get to meet the person God has for them. God's going to give them choices; He doesn't usually assign you a mate. Within His guidelines, you can choose the person who's right for you and He will honor that.

Before you make up your mind completely about whether this person is going to be your husband or your wife, you need to have a question-and-answer session. The first question you need to ask is this: "What first attracted you to me?" Second question: "What do I add to your life?" See what they say. Another very important question: "When do you enjoy me the most?" Listen to what your prospective mate has to say.

What are some character traits and qualities a person should look for before saying, "I'm going to marry that person"? What are some character flaws or qualities you should watch for?

Honesty or dishonesty. Personality. Generosity or stinginess. Mental stability or instability. Whether or not that person finishes what he or she starts. Whether he or she is easily swayed. Whether that person has clear goals. Integrity. Faithfulness. The ability to love. Commitment. Responsibility. Dependability. Flexibility and compassion. Faith. Principles. Respect for you and for oneself.

If it's a man, the woman needs to know whether that man desires to work. Whether you both would like to have children. Sometimes people just assume things. When I married my wife, I told her point-blank I didn't want any children. I love my children now. I had a change of heart.

You need to know whether your prospective spouse is committed to Christ. You should know something about the person's family. You need to know something about their views on issues that are important to you. That's why you need to communicate.

Women, never marry a man who tries to dominate you. A dominated woman will never reach her full potential. Men, never marry a woman who manipulates you. A woman who manipulates the man will keep that man from ever reaching the potential that God has for him. God doesn't want any of us to be dominated, controlled, or manipulated.

When a person wants you to be just like him or her in every way, that controls your thinking. Not all women are alike and not all men are alike. But men and women are basically different. They see things differently. God doesn't want us to become just like our husband or just like our wife. There needs to be a balance there. Let our differences draw us together instead of driving us apart.

That's why He made you different. You see, when the Bible says you become one, that doesn't mean you lose your identity. It does not mean that you can't think unless your spouse is around. There's nothing worse than talking to a man who can't make decisions. But there are some things you have to check with your spouse.

Now, the choice that you make, not only is it a permanent commitment in the eyes of the civil law, but God is going to consider it permanent too. Suppose that, although you know what the Word has to say, you decide to marry someone who is not a believer. You decide to skip the six months of counseling too, and figure that your partner will be born again sooner or later. God's going to hold you accountable for what you know. And when you marry that person, society will recognize it, and so will God. Even if you later realize it was a mistake, you are married to that person for life.

My mother used to say, "If you make your bed, you lie in it." All single people need to ask themselves, before they get married: Do I want to spend the rest of my life with him or her?

But suppose you've carefully chosen a mate. When do you get married? I believe that a man needs to get married when he's ready to die for that woman, and when he is ready to wash her in the Word. By "washing in the Word," I mean when he's ready to teach her, when he's able to teach her. The first man, Adam, taught the first woman, Eve, all that he knew. He taught her the names of all things—animals, fish, trees, and fruit. In the third chapter of Genesis Eve spoke the word of God that she had learned from her husband, Adam, to the serpent.

When you have a woman who is on fire for God and a man who is not on fire for God, you're going to have an imbalance. The man is supposed to be the priest of the home. He needs to be ready. He should be able to teach his wife. If you're not at that point, maybe you're not ready to get married. If you're not ready to die for your wife, how can you lay down your life for her day by day?

I think that a woman is ready to get married when she's ready to submit to her husband the way the Bible says she is to submit. Marriage is like the Church. It tells us that in Ephesians. Jesus Christ is the head of the body, of the Church. Jesus is there for us, and that's the way we should be for our wives. And as the Church submits to Jesus, that's the way a woman should submit to her husband. Submission is something a woman allows to happen. And submission is not domination, either.

Before anyone gets married, there needs to be a formal announcement so that everyone can know that these two people have been spoken for. Then the pastor can say, "They stood up and said before this congregation and before God that they love one another and they are intended for one another, and therefore I'm telling you, 'Don't interfere in this relationship.' "

We need to treat each other, and the institution of marriage, and the preparation for it, with respect.

Reflections

1. Dating is serious business.

2. Singles should not be dating each other unless it is part of the process of finding a mate.

3. Don't continue in a relationship if there's no possibility of marriage.

4. Sexual temptations are one of the biggest problems singles have when dating.

5. Until a person knows Jesus Christ, he or she will never experience the real love that God intended for a man and a woman.

6. The glamour of sex will lead to sin, even death.

7. People change when they are together for long periods of time.

8. Mature relationship energize you and make you feel good about yourself.

9. Real love is conceived when two people enter emotional intimacy—not dependency.

10. Real, mature love is almost like music.

Chapter 4

Separate From the World

Madonna is one of the most popular women in the world just now, and one of the most influential. She told her fans to vote for Clinton. Some people attribute Clinton's election to the influence she has in this country. And this woman, who starred in her own book of pornography, bears the name of the mother of Christ.

How many people are imitating Madonna, especially young people! Some psychiatrists have even said that she's a good role model. And the majority of people in this country seem to go along with all this perverted stuff, accepting it if not buying Madonna's tapes and book.

Sin is certainly alluring. Madonna's very name reminds us of what people are ignoring—biblical role models—as they follow the way of the world. We could hardly pick a better example than Madonna to express the dichotomy in our society. And yet Madonna too will fade from the scene before long as people seek some new sensation.

However, just as shocking as Madonna's antics is the fact that a lot of Christians think that things are not all that bad. We're like Lot's family in Sodom. There's hell all around us, but we have gotten used to it. Yet the gap is widening, and some people are trying to get by with compromise.

Some Christians are saying that it's too hard to stay pure. They think they can get drunk now and then; they think they can sleep around just a little bit as long as they don't hurt anyone. It does hurt. The wages of sin are always death. Sin always has the same result.

It doesn't matter what the majority say. Homosexuality is also wrong. Abortion is also wrong—even if 43% vote for it. Today you have to be hooked up and connected to Jesus. Nothing else will do. We're not going to soften the Word. We're not going to tell people that compromising with the world is enough. The truth is that sin is still deadly. The truth remains that Jesus is the Way. There is no other way of life, only the way of death—no matter what Madonna says.

Some people try to compromise with sin by saying that Madonna's book is liberating women. There's nothing wrong with fantasizing, they say. We're not talking about innocent daydreams, thinking about what you're going to do this weekend. We're talking about fantasies of sin: bestiality, having sex with children, anal sex, oral sex, sadomasochism. This is not liberation. This is enslavement. It took hundreds of years to abolish slavery in this country, and now some of us are enslaving ourselves to something far worse. As horrible and wrong as the institution of slavery was, it did not drag slaves into hell. The kind of slavery Madonna and her like are offering is an eternal slavery, unless you grab hold of the Savior.

We need to keep our focus on God. Sometimes people concentrate on their needs. They get their needs and demands mixed up. They start concentrating on their happiness. But when we talk about the Lord, we're really talking about joy, not happiness. There's joy in the Lord. What we need is His salvation, His mercy, His joy.

Ecclesiastes tells us that when you please God, God will give you knowledge, wisdom and happiness. The things of this world cannot make us happy. The kind of self-indulgence exhibited by Madonna cannot make you happy. God gives us the desires of our heart, but we can't focus our attention on this world. Jesus is our Source—our Source of joy, our Source for everything.

Now, when you start talking like that, some people will say that you're weak-minded. We have to be prepared to stand. In our society, the people who call on the name of Jesus have to know who they are in Him. We have to know what we stand for, because everything's going to come and shake us.

Those who go to college will find pressure to compromise; people will be telling you things that are contradictory to the Word. At almost any job you'll find people contradicting the Word. You turn on the television, and almost everything contradicts the Word of God. You wouldn't want someone to get naked and come into your house and have sex in front of you. You wouldn't allow it. But turn on your television and it's the same thing. We have to have willpower to turn this stuff off, and not allow it to get into our spirit or into our children's minds.

We need God. We don't need filth for entertainment every night, or even every week, or at all. We do have real needs, and it's up to us, the Body of Christ, to show the world Jesus. The world needs Jesus.

How do we keep aware of each other's needs? By communicating and being sensitive to each other. Matthew 23:11-12 tells us: "The greatest among you will be your servant. For whoever exalts himself will be humbled, and whoever humbles himself will be exalted."

One way husbands and wives can stay sensitive to or aware of each other's needs is to be servants to each other, to have a servant's attitude. In our church, we have one sister who is in charge of hospitality. When we're having a banquet and we have speakers, she watches the tables. She serves, she watches and if there's a need she tries to fill it, along with others who help.

In the relationship between husband and wife, you can become aware of each other's needs by having a servant's attitude. If there's a need, you want to fill it. This doesn't mean filling demands. The world is trying to get husbands and wives to make demands on each other. We shouldn't be demanding things of each other. But we have needs we can communicate in a humble way. We can look for each other's needs and just fill them.

I used to carry all the money in my pocket. I used to carry the checkbook; I used to handle everything. When my wife wanted some money, she'd have to come and ask me. Then one day, twenty-some years ago, she asked for some money—only a dollar. "Honey," she said, "I would like to have a dollar."

And I said, "For what?" And I realized that we had outgrown that kind of relationship. She didn't need me to be a big daddy to her. I had to adjust myself to that need. Now she keeps the money! But the point I'm trying to make is that needs come up in our lives, and if we don't address them, we can have big problems.

Learning how to give brings about that servant kind of attitude. Some people want to exalt themselves over each other. The Bible says that if you exalt yourself, you're going to be humbled. And if God brings you down, you're really going to be brought down.

When you develop a servant's attitude in your marriage, you learn how to do three things in the way of ministering to one another. You learn how to fill moment-to-moment needs. It's almost automatic. If you know something's wrong, you're there to help. You're there to give of yourself.

Second, you give understanding to each other. You learn how to understand. I told my wife, "Honey, you should be able to tell me anything. Anything." If she told me there was a big old boogey man outside, I would believe her.

Some husbands would say, "Look, you need to go to sleep." Some wives may not want to share much with their husbands because their husbands think that they're weird or crazy. You should be able to share anything, to have a type of understanding.

Third, we learn to be aware of our responsibility to fill needs. I need at least to be alert to the needs of my mate.

When we meet each other's needs, that action itself demonstrates love. For a lot of men, it is a humbling experience to say, "I'm wrong." It's humbling for a lot of women, too, because there's a battle between the sexes going on. "I've got to have my way," people are saying, "and if I don't have my way, it's going to be no way." Then the needs are not being met in that relationship. And what happens?

You get resentful. You want your needs met. And you start looking elsewhere for that.

God told Israel not to run after foreign gods. Well, your spiritual walk with your spouse is almost like your relationship with Jesus.

How careful are we when speaking to God? Yet you can say the wrong thing to your spouse, and sometimes not even know it. We need the sensitivity of the Holy Spirit to guide us in our marital relationships.

But we need to do some looking on our own, to be aware of our mate's needs. So I asked the women in my congregation to name some of the biggest needs in their lives.

One of the greatest needs a woman has in a marriage is to know that she's loved. Once she knows that she's loved for who she is, and appreciated, you don't have to have any money. You don't have to have a bunch of things.

The next one is security—not just to be secure in the physical sense, but to be secure in her husband's love, to know you're not going to run out on her after she has two or three children for you.

Women want to be valued for who they are.

Respect is another major need. So are fidelity, honesty, trust and affection—women like to be touched. Love demands touching.

How do we show our wives that we love them? God shows husbands how to love their wives: as Christ loved the Church. Do you give her a can-opener for her birthday? Do you tell her, "I told you I love you last anniversary. Why do you want to hear it again this anniversary?" "I bought you flowers six years ago. Why do I have to keep spending money on those types of things?"

What do we say when our wives ask, "Honey, why don't you call me sometimes?"

Do we respond, "Call you! What do I have to call you for? I'm busy at work." Why? Because women like to know that they're loved.

How do women like for their husbands to show them that they're loved? Some mentioned gifts. Travel: it shows you care if you want her with you when you travel. You don't even have to leave the city. Just take her away from the house, away from the kids, away from the hustle and bustle, just go for a walk. They need to know they're loved. One woman said, "If you don't love us during the day, we don't want you to need us at night." If we love them all day, at night the response will be, "Yes, honey, from the bottom of my heart."

Husbands can show respect by listening. Sometimes we'll say, "You don't give me a chance to listen." But we don't really listen. If our wives want to see if we're listening, all they have to do is ask us, "Repeat to me what I said to you."

When is the last time you told your wife that you appreciate her—and not when you're sitting at the table looking at a good dinner. How about going home to find that your wife didn't feel like cleaning the house, and saying, "Honey, I appreciate you"? That gives her security.

How else do we give our wives security? If a man doesn't know who he is, how can his wife follow him? For a woman to live with a man who doesn't know where he's going gives her a certain amount of insecurity. If you're a man who leaves his job every two months because "God called you to another job," your family begins to lose their sense of security. Especially if they're hearing every six weeks, "God showed me, honey. We're going to get rich this time. I promise you." But if you know who you are, and your wife can have confidence in you, you can go places.

Women also feel secure when we tell them they're pretty. Women want to be pretty, feel pretty, and act pretty. The average woman likes pretty things. She likes soft things. She likes bubble-baths. She likes perfume. She likes nail polish. And if you find a woman who's not like that, something happened in her childhood where she was made to feel ugly. And it's our job to help her feel pretty, to regain the femininity God designed for her. Femininity and masculinity is a learned behavior. Masculinity and femininity are learned not something we are born with.

Women get security from being touched by their husbands. They like for us to hold their hands, and not just when it's time to go to bed. That's where most men go wrong. They get very affectionate when the lights go out. But what about all day? My wife says, if your husband doesn't open the door for you, and leaves you sitting in the car, when he gets ready to go to bed at night, he'll figure out where he left you. He may not miss you till it's bedtime, but you sit right there. Don't dare open the door for yourself. And when he gets ready to go to bed at night, he's going to say, "Hmmm. I'm lonely. Where's my wife?

She must be in the car." Women like affection. And they like us to hold the door open for them.

One wife said, "When I was dating my husband, he would always open the door for me. And right after we got married, he would just slide in. I thought, 'I'm not putting up with this trash anymore. You open the door for me, I might bless you.' When I insisted on it, he started opening the door for me. Now we sleep holding hands. I woke up one night, and we were asleep holding hands. I had to get up.

" 'Where are you going?' he asked.

" 'I'm just going to the bathroom,' I answered. 'I'll be right back. I promise you. Just hold your dream right there.' If you want your husband to hold your hand, and he doesn't like to, start holding his. If he rejects you, don't worry about it. Just keep holding his hand. Be faithful."

Husbands want their wives to be faithful—not just in the sense of desiring only him, but in showing respect. That's fidelity too. The surest way to emasculate a man is to talk down to him in front of other people or in front of his children. It shows that you don't respect him, and he will lose respect for you.

We men need to learn how to be affectionate, how to express the loving feeling we have toward our wives. You have to smother them with affection early in the morning. You have to smother them with affection early in the afternoon. You have to smother them with affection late in the afternoon, early in the night, late at night. Then start all over again. Affection helps to create an atmosphere for romance, too. If you're not affectionate, if you don't meet that woman's need for affection, you're not going to have the atmosphere for romance and intimacy.

Sometimes women see affection and sex going hand in hand. You almost can't have one without the other. There are a lot of men who want to have the other without affection, and that's where they go wrong.

Women also have a need for conversation or communication. Women feel united with their husbands when they can converse with them. Women speak 75,000 words a day. Men speak 25,000 words a day. Women have that need to talk. Men, if you go to work and speak your 24,500 words and come back home with only 500 words left, and she stays home and speaks only 5,000, she has 70,000 words left. What do you think's going to happen? You come home. You say, "Hello, how you doin'? Oh, what's for dinner?" And you've used a few already, right?

And she has 70,000 words left. And she's going around like a lion: "Talk to me! Talk to me! Talk to me!" And your 500 words are over with, and you find yourself going, "Um-hmm. Whatever you say. It's fine with me. Uh-huh. Whatever you want to do is fine. Um-hmm." When you run out of your 500 words, remember, you've got to dig up some words somewhere else, or save some when you're on your job.

Does your wife ever say, "You can talk to everybody else, but you never talk to me"? Maybe you already used up your 25,000 words talking to everybody else.

My wife talks me to sleep sometimes.

"Honey," I'll say, "honestly, I'm listening to what you're saying."

"You don't listen..."

"I *am* listening, honey; I'm listening. Just tell me again. What was it you said?"

"Even if you run out of words, pastor," one of the women in my congregation told me, "if you give your wife attention, let her know you're listening to what she's saying, she will appreciate that."

Wives feel united, connected to their husbands when they can communicate with their husband. Not talking to your wife can cause you to grow apart.

Wives also have a need for honesty and openness. Openness brings trust and increases trust. A lot of times men don't think this is important. But it's important to our wives. And if we can't fill that need, it makes her feel insecure, as though maybe something's wrong with her, or maybe she's not doing what she needs to be doing, because you're not honest. You're not open. Sometimes it's very difficult for men to be open. I'm not even open with my natural brothers and sisters the way I should be. Men are always afraid to make themselves vulnerable. Some men worship their masculinity and become emotionally constipated. They hold everything in because the world has said that it's a sign of weakness for a man to show emotion. That's one of the biggest lies ever told.

"Most women have a problem because men won't open up," one woman said to me. "You feel like you're talking to a brick wall."

That's why opening up is important. You should be putting bricks in the wall, building together, not having a wall to keep each other apart.

I like the relationship my wife and I have in the church. My wife and I, we talk. Most couples I see in the ministry, the woman is always dominating the man. Whenever you have a woman who comes up and says, "I'm going to take over now," that leaves the man with nothing. We can't allow the worldly mentality to come in and bring separation between the sexes.

On the other hand, you can get so spiritual that you won't be able to communicate with your spouse. You can say, "Thank you, Jesus" all you want to, but let me tell you something: if you can't communicate with the one God has put beside you, you are going to feel an empty void. That's why we have so many divorces.

Sometimes communication between spouses is a problem because you feel like you're speaking two different languages. Sometimes women hear in a language that is more emotional. Men tend to hear information. That doesn't mean it's wrong. It means that God has made us this way. I can recount numerous conversations I've had with my wife.

"Honey, this is the way I feel."

"No, you don't really feel that way. You feel..."

"Wait a minute! That's really how I feel."

"No, this is the way you feel!"

Or I'll say, "This is the way I see it, you know, and there's nothing else there. There's nothing else there."

"No, there is something else there."

I'm stating information, which is all I want to say, but my wife will interpret it in an emotional way. And there may be emotions involved. I just wasn't intending to communicate them, maybe wasn't even aware of them, but my wife picks up on them.

Is one wrong and one right? Not necessarily. Maybe one person is just looking at the problem from a different point of view. In the spirit realm, women are normally a little sharper. Is that to say that women are more spiritual? No, it's just that they see things differently. And women have to understand that if God has made men different, it doesn't mean that women are supposed to make men into women. Perceiving things emotionally is not bad, and looking strictly at information is not bad. They each have their place, and together there's a balance.

Women have more needs than men, and a lot of times women will go a little extra distance to make sure those needs are being met. You get a bunch of women together who each have 75,000 words to say, and they will talk each other to death.

If a wife has her needs met, that will be reflected in the way she relates to her husband. Even the need for financial security is reflected. It's very important to them. I believe that financial stability has a direct relationship with your sexual life.

That's tied into family commitment. Women like to know that the husband is going to be a good husband and father. They like to know that he's going to be a friend to his wife.

Now, what are some of the needs men have? Understanding. Respect. Support. Patience. Trust and faithfulness. Companionship. Oneness with the wife. Proper communication. Maturity. Sex.

The number-one need, I believe, for most men in a marital relationship is sexual fulfillment. A lot of husbands turn into different creatures if that need is not met. There are some people who don't understand why they have problems in their relationship.

Another thing men need is to have fun with someone. Women often don't want to do anything men want to do. If he wants to watch football, you don't want to watch it. If he wants to go fishing, you don't want to do that either. But every man has a need for someone to have fun with.

That's why your wife needs to be your best friend—to be somebody you can talk to and laugh with and have fun with. Friendship is the foundation for love. A lot of friendships begin when people are looking to have their needs met. A husband and wife need to keep meeting each other's needs, and to be friends. There need to be mutual interests. Some wives never do anything with their husbands.

I love being around other men and laughing and talking. I love throwing horseshoes. I love having fun. But friendship needs to extend to your wife. And the wife needs to know that. Some women are a joy to be around. You love being around them. You like talking to them. You laugh with them. You feel comfortable around them. The next thing you know, friendship develops, because needs are being fulfilled.

A man also has a need, I believe, to be with an attractive woman, his wife, in public. A man has an ego. When he goes out somewhere, and he takes his wife along, he wants people to notice his wife. That makes him look good.

Women have a need to be attractive too. When my wife is going out by herself, she'll put on different clothes and put on more makeup. I used to ask her, "Who are you going to meet?"

She explained that she usually runs into someone I know, or someone she used to work with. She said, "You don't want me going out looking like a hag." She wanted to look good for me, as my wife, even when I'm not around.

Then when another man says to me, "I saw your wife the other day," I know he's saying she was very attractive. Men have a need to hear that.

My wife says that women need to look good all the time, not just outside. She's tried to cultivate that in our children. Erica used to sleep in T-shirts, and that used to drive my wife crazy. Erica would get my T-shirt or her brother's T-shirt, and my wife used to fuss and say, "Girl, I buy you nice stuff. Why don't you use it?" I told her, "Buy her the kind of stuff you like." So she began to buy her pajamas, and lace stuff, and now she knows what she's supposed to do. But if you let your little girl sleep in daddy's T-shirts and old beat-up socks, she'll grow up thinking that it's acceptable. When she gets married, she'll just put on any old thing.

My wife told Erica, "I feel that my husband is too good for me to go to bed with a raggedy gown, and a rag on my head."

When a wife looks good for her mate in public, it makes her husband feel good. Men are sight-oriented. But if your wife is unattractive in public, something goes out from you, goes away from you. But a man needs to help his wife be the kind of wife he wants her to be. Buy her the kind of clothes you would like to see her wearing. Eventually, you'll be looking at what you want to look at.

Another thing a man needs is for his wife to support him. No man wants a woman to fight him all the time. It does something to a man. It does something to his ego. Sometimes a couple will disagree. There's nothing wrong with disagreeing. But constantly fighting and saying, "You don't know what you're doing. I don't go along with that"—eventually there will be a part of him that will not respond to his wife the way she would like. The Holy Spirit has a way of dealing with us, to let us know that we need to be at peace. He will let us know if we're fostering division.

When we got ready to move to Texas, my wife told me, "Honey, there's no way I'm going to Texas. I am not going to that God-forsaken place."

"Honey, wait a minute," I said. "God told me to go to Texas."

"Do you think I'm going down there with cowboys and armadillos and people who drive around with guns in the back of their cars! I'm not going to a place like that."

Finally, she got a group of ladies in Europe to pray for me—ladies all over Germany, all over Europe, I mean hundreds of women. They had a prayer chain going. They thought I was possessed by a demon, you know, to go to someplace called Texas. And we went to a charismatic conference up in the mountains, and all these women came around me, hugging me and saying, "Oh, brother," as if there were something wrong with me. My wife wasn't supporting me. And something inside me died.

I came to Texas twice. The first time, I rode on the bus all over San Antonio, and I went back and said, "Honey, this is the place."

"You've lost it," she said.

When I came back again, I rented a car, and rode all over the place again. And I bought a house. That really did it. After we came here, it was still bad. Let me tell you, when your wife does not support you, you can barely function. And then if your wife tells you that you missed what God was trying to tell you, you feel like you did miss it.

But when God touched her heart, when she finally came aboard, she came full force. My wife is my strongest supporter and stands with me in everything that God gives me to do. If a woman supports her man, there's no telling what he might be able to accomplish. No devil in hell can come up against you if your wife is with you.

Now, understand: if you have an opinion, and your husband has an opinion, you still need to state your opinion. And you need to hear his opinion.

But it has to be with respect. Another need a man has is for his wife to respect and admire him. The man is supposed to love his wife as Christ loves the Church. But the Word says that the woman needs to respect the man. Respect is very, very important to a man. God has made us that way. It's not that we're trying to be something we're not. But the man needs to be honored as head of the household.

It seems that a lot of men are leaving their families primarily for one reason, that the man has felt a lot of pressure on him to be the provider, which he should be, but all he does is provide. He doesn't get involved with the family the way he should. Consequently, the woman sees that man as just a person to bring in the bacon. We need to involve ourselves with our wives and children.

Instead of just bringing home the food and money, we have to remember that we're fathers and husbands, not just providers.

Think back to your own family. Can you see the man saying, "I've done my job. I'm going to sit in this chair and watch TV. Don't bother me. Just go with your mama"? We have to get out of that attitude.

We have a responsibility as husbands and wives to live up to our roles, and to encourage each other to live up to our roles. Sometimes women treat their husbands like children. Sometimes we talk to one another as if we were children. We need to learn how to talk to our husbands and wives as adult to adult. We need some maturity, because we have an adult job to do for our families. We're warriors defending them.

Refelctions

1. We need to keep our focus on God.

2. Learning how to give brings about that servant kind of attitude.

3. One of the greatest needs a woman has in a marriage is to know that she's loved.

4. Women get security from being touched by their husbands.

5. The surest way to emasculate a man is to talk down to him in front of other people or in front of his children.

6. Sometimes women see affection and sex going hand in hand.

7. Sometimes it's very difficult for men to be open.

8. Women have more needs than men, and a lot of times women will go a little extra distance to make sure those needs are being met.

9. When a wife looks good for her mate in public, it makes her husband feel good.

10. No devil in hell can come up against you if your wife is with you.

Chapter 5

Resisting Attacks on the Family

When Clinton was running for president, he said he felt that a thirteen-year-old girl should not have to get her parents' permission before having an abortion. This man is now President of the United States, and he thinks that abortion is a matter between a thirteen-year-old girl and her doctor, that the parents should stay out of it.

Earlier we looked at the idea of redefining the family. This idea of Clinton's is another attempt at that, another attack on the family. It's saying that thirteen-year-olds are mature enough to decide whether to have surgery; that thirteen-year-olds are mature enough to make a life-and-death decision for a baby they have conceived; that parents may not exercise authority over their minor children living at home; that the parents' only responsibility is to pay for any medical bills that occur as the result of an abortion. That last item occurs all too often. There's a lady in Virginia, a born-again Christian lady named Eileen Roberts, who started an organization called Mothers Against Minors' Abortions. Her own daughter had an abortion without Eileen's knowledge, and the abortion did plenty of physical damage and left emotional scars too. Eileen and her husband had to pay thousands of dollars in medical bills for their daughter to take care of the damage done by the abortionist.

So what is the President's idea really saying? That the family is not legal, and should not be, what it used to be. Parents may not interfere with their teenagers' decisions. All the parents must do is pay for the mess. This is redefining the family. This is an attack on the family.

The law and society are telling us that the Christian family is obsolete, and on its way to being illegal. The law now allows children to sue their parents.

We now have men marrying men, women marrying women. I saw a newspaper headline: "Wedding Bells Ring for Beauty Who Used to Be a Man." There was a wedding ceremony in Montreal for a man and a "woman" who had had sex-change surgery to turn the person from male to female. The so-called reverend who performed the ceremony said, "They deserve to be happy." The "bride's" sister promised to make their life complete by being a surrogate mother for them.

That gives you an idea of why people are trying to redefine the family. They have the idea that everyone deserves to be happy, no matter what it takes. If it means that a thirteen-year-old can have sex with her boyfriend, and have an abortion when she gets pregnant—all right, if that's what it takes to make her happy, then the parents have to butt out. If it means a man can try to have himself turned into a woman and get "married" and have children, then that's okay. The law will allow it.

An awful lot of television programs are saying the same thing. They go against traditional values. They teach that adultery, homosexuality, and any other perversion is okay if that's what you need to make you happy.

Of course, the people who are trying to redefine the family and to abolish the Christian model of the family have not ignored the schools. A colorful picture book called *Daddy's Roommate* depicts the homosexual lifestyle as normal, and includes drawings of two homosexuals in bed together. New York City recently tried to make this book, and another called *Heather Has Two Mommies*, part of the public school curriculum.

These are attacks on the family. These are attacks on your family. What are we going to do about it?

Some people say that because Christ went meekly to the cross, like a lamb to the slaughter, we do not have to oppose evil. Christ also drove the money changers out of the temple, and told His disciples, "I have not come to bring peace but a sword." There is a time for righteous anger.

Christians acting together have gotten hotels to get rid of all the porn movies because people complained and stopped doing business there. Churches stopped using the facilities for conferences. People stopped telling out-of-town visitors to use the hotel. And it made a difference. And it's an important difference, if you look at it from a biblical point of view. The world tells us that pornography is an individual's own private business. The Bible tells us that parents are supposed to defend their children against evil. When your teenage daughter is out with her friends some evening, do you want her encountering some guy who's been staying at the local hotel watching porn movies? We have to oppose evil.

And if we're going to oppose evil, then we have to strengthen our own families. That means unity. That means that a husband and wife have to work together and support each other, even when they have disagreements. We have to have a Christian way of handling disagreements in our families and in our marriages.

Because men and women are different, sometimes they are going to disagree. You're not going to see things just alike. Problems occur when you go from disagreement into conflict. Then you have people who don't want to talk to one another. You have people sleeping in different parts of the house to get away from each other. If you see your disagreements turning into conflicts, you have to go right to the next step, which is resolution. Someone has to take the initiative. If no one moves toward resolution, you're going to be building walls, causing separation, and the devil's going to come up and rip your relationship apart.

Now, it's hard to move into resolution, because most of the time people's pride gets in the way. To be safe, if you can't move into resolution, it's best sometimes to just move back into disagreement—to acknowledge that you have this difference, that you can't agree on something, but you can agree that you're not going to fight about it and that you're not going to stop loving each other over it. "We just have a disagreement. Okay, I see your point, you know, and I understand that, and I disagree with you, but I appreciate what you said." Then you can go on. There's nothing wrong with disagreeing over something. But if you get into conflict over something and don't move forward to resolution or backward at least to disagreement, you can't get out of it.

Once at a marriage seminar, a man got up and said, "You know what? My wife and I have been married for thirty years, and we have never had a quarrel." Everybody was just sitting still, waiting to see what was going to be said about that.

Another man got up. He said, "Well, that's pretty good that you and your wife have been married for thirty years and you've never had a quarrel, but you've missed the best part of being married."

"What's that?" the first man asked.

"Making up." So it depends on how you look at things. Some people say that if you don't quarrel, you have a good marriage. That's not necessarily true. By the mere fact that you are different, you are going to have some disagreements.

Marriage is very exciting. It's very mysterious. And it can even be very frightening. To me it's like dancing on a tightrope together. Sometimes you let go, and if somebody falls, you are going to get hurt. You have to be in harmony.

You have to have fellowship—one of the main reasons people get married is for fellowship. Fellowship means spending time together, close association, doing things together.

Communication is also fellowship. If you have problems talking to one another, you will have problems having fellowship. Poor communication can destroy future communication, and bring up some other problems. If you can't communicate with your spouse right now (or if you're planning on getting married and are not able to communicate with your fiancé) you're going to have problems in the future.

You have to work at learning to communicate. Most men don't know how to make themselves understood to women. On the other hand, most women don't know how to communicate with men. You can be just talking to one another but not communicating anything. There will be no real fellowship there because no one will understand what the other is trying to communicate.

Communication is an art, something that must be learned. And effective communication, the kind of communication that brings about understanding, creates intimacy, which leads to romance. A lot of people never get to romance because there is no real communication.

We've considered the fact that for most women, language is an emotional experience. If a wife tells her husband that his shoes don't go with his clothes, he'll change his shoes and go out. If a husband tells his wife that her shoes don't look right with her clothes, she doesn't think, "I need to change my shoes." What she hears is "You're dumb," or "You're fat," or "That dress looks ugly." If a husband doesn't know that language is an emotional experience for his wife, then he can open his mouth and put the kiss of death on their relationship, because he doesn't know how to talk to his wife.

Some men think they can say anything to their wives, and when the wife reacts, the man says, "What in the world is wrong? What did I say? All I said was, 'You look stupid with that on.' That's all I said. I mean, why don't you just take it off?" The next thing you know, not only is she quiet, but she has a hard time sitting at the table with him, much less going to bed with him.

We mentioned too that language is usually interpreted by men as information. He needs to understand what you mean. If you want him to put his arm around you, you can't just say, "It's chilly in here." He takes that as information. You want him to turn the heat up. He may not even like that idea, because the heating bill has been so high. Now there's something that men will take personally—the man hears that his wife is chilly, and he takes that to mean, "She doesn't think I'm a good provider." And all the wife wanted was for him to hold her.

Or a man goes home, and says to his wife, "Sister Jones sure looked nice in church today."

She's not going to hear that Sister Jones looked nice. She's going to hear "I looked bad. You liked what she had on, and you didn't even notice me."

So we have different languages being spoken. That's why talking may not be effective communication. Good communication takes time. You have to learn each other's ideas and attitudes and ways of doing things. It's hard work all the time.

Of the conversations men have with women, only seven percent of it is understood. Suppose the husband says, "It's time to go now. It's eleven. I don't want to be late for church. What's the problem? Your makeup? Well, can't you do that in the car?" The woman may not even be hearing what he's saying. She is focusing more on something else.

Thirty-eight percent of what's communicated is the way you say it. That's where thirty-eight percent of her attention is focused. The husband is concerned about being late for church and maybe all she's thinking is, "Don't raise your voice at me."

Now suppose he says, "Is it all right to go now?"

She may answer, "Oh, yeah, honey. It's time to go now."

Fifty-five percent of the conversation is focused on nonverbals. Men, when you're talking to your wife, it's important to give her some gestures, to touch her, to look at her, to give her your undivided attention, because she looks at that and she hears more of the nonverbals than what you're saying.

We need to know these things because men and women can get preoccupied with doing something else, and you can cause your spouse to get angry with you and you won't even know why. Many of the personal problems we have in our marriages may only be communication problems.

We need to be on guard. We need to be guarding each other. There's a saying: "You always hurt the one you love." We're in a position where it's very easy to hurt the people we're married to. We need to guard them from ourselves.

At the same time, we need to expect each other's love. We can't always be questioning it. We can't always be asking, "Why did he say that? What did he mean by that? Maybe he doesn't love me any more." We need to cut the other person some slack. I make mistakes. My wife makes mistakes. We can't take everything personally.

We have to look out for each other. The husband and wife cannot afford to be down at the same time. It's the husband's responsibility to notice when his wife is down. If she is, he needs to be up; he needs to help her. "Honey, is there anything I can do for you?" He may have had a rough day himself, but he has to support her. The moment you allow both of you to be down at the same time, you open the door for the devil to come in.

Partnership means you are on the same team. A lot of husbands and wives fight against one another and compete against one another. But two people who combine their abilities, their assets and their talents share the profits and gains in life. If things go bad, they go bad for both of you. If you're blessed, that means you're both blessed. Being in a husband-and-wife partnership means putting each other first (after God). Then you will have a solid, godly team that will enable your family to resist the attacks of the devil and experience spiritual victory.

Reflections

1. The law and society are telling us that the Christian family is obsolete and on it's way to being illegal.

2. Because men and women are different, sometimes they are going to disagree.

3. You have to work at learning to communicate.

4. Communication is an art; something that must be learned.

5. Partnership means you are on the same team.

Chapter 6

Society vs. the Family

In September 1992, Dr. Dobson of Focus on the Family sent a letter to his supporters concerning the crisis facing the family in our society today. I think that what he said is worth reflecting on.

He said that in 1992 and 1993 there would be programs on television that would work to utterly destroy the family. He said that there's a diabolical attack coming at us from the enemy, but it's happening through NBC, ABC and CBS, who are competing to attract and keep the attention of the people who are viewing television. They do that with raw sex and raw violence.

One program Dr. Dobson cited was *Eyewitness Video*. It features actual footage of incredibly violent and bloody events—not re-enactments. One episode, he said, shows a cop being kicked, stabbed and shot to death. Another depicts a Texas police officer killing a suspected drug dealer. Yet another shows a speeding truck hitting a pedestrian as the driver attempts to escape from the police. The effect is sickening. Later, police pour bullets into the cab of the truck, killing the fugitive. In the final scene, he is shown hanging out of the window with blood gushing from his head. Other upcoming segments include a pregnant woman suspended from a window of a burning building, photographs of mutilated murder victims, an airplane crashing into a crowd, and a man preparing to kill himself on television.

Yes, this is real life, and it's horrible. Many of us have witnessed one kind of disaster or another, or have lived through combat, and witnessing one or two incidents like that is enough to last you a lifetime. Now, we're being invited to fill our minds with it every week.

Why? For our own good? Of course not. It's because people will tune in to something sensational. The broadcasters are making money on it.

Dr. Dobson also mentioned a new program called *Love and War*. In an early episode, said Dr. Dobson, the lead male character asks his female counterpart, "Your condom or mine?" One of them claims to have had more sexual partners than the Pope but fewer than Jimmy Swaggert. The message is that they need "protection"—condoms. And that was their first date. Supposedly this kind of programming *is* for our own good. But it's a lie. It's telling people that condoms will protect them from disease. The truth is that condoms often fail to prevent pregnancy, and that they are not foolproof against AIDS and other diseases. That's not "safe." Sin never is.

US magazine in August 1992 carried a cover story called "Sex and Entertainment—How Far Can It Go?" Their lead story featured this headline: "Welcome to the New Sexual Revolution." Most of the shows involve the sexual antics of the main characters, who are often hounded by right-wing fanatics. Guess who the right-wing fanatics are: Christians. People who dare to say that it's wrong to deviate from God's plan for sex and marriage. People who dare to live as though morals are important.

But are we living that way? Just a few years ago, it was not possible to show a homosexual couple on television without inciting a storm of protest. Now, homosexuals are prominent on television. It is amazing just how rapidly America has forgotten its moral underpinnings. That's partly our fault. We kept quiet for so long that we were no longer at the center of society. We got left out on the right wing.

This treatment of Christians extends to anyone in politics who still has some principles. Yes, there are a few of those people left. Look at how Dan Quayle was ridiculed for his speech about the family in crisis. He mentioned the television character Murphy Brown as an example of television working against the family. Most commentators spoke as though this speech were the stupidest speech ever made in history.

What he had to say was not stupid. He said that the failure of our families is hurting America deeply. He said that when families fall, society falls. He blamed the anarchy and lack of structure in our inner cities on cracks in the family foundation.

Quayle said that children need love and discipline; that they need mothers and fathers. He said that a welfare check is not a husband, that the state is not a father. He said that marriage is probably the best antipoverty program of all, because only 5.7% of families headed by married couples are in poverty, while 33.4% of families headed by a single mother are in poverty.

"Where there are no mature, responsible men around to teach boys how to become good men," Dan Quayle said, "gangs serve in their place. In fact, gangs have become a surrogate family for much of a generation of inner city boys. I recently visited with some former gang members in Albuquerque, New Mexico. In a private meeting they told me why they had joined gangs. These teenage boys said that gangs gave them a sense of security. They made them feel wanted and useful. They got support from their friends, and they said it was like having a family. Like family. Unfortunately, that says it all. The system perpetuates itself as these young men father children whom they have no intention of caring for by women whose welfare checks support them. Teenage girls mired in the same hopelessness lack sufficient motive to say no to this trap. Answers to our problems won't be easy. We can start by dismantling a welfare system that encourages dependency and subsidizes broken families. We can attach conditions such as school attendance or work to welfare. We can limit the time a recipient gets benefits. We can stop penalizing marriage for welfare mothers. We can enforce child support payments. Ultimately, however, marriages are a moral issue that requires cultural consensus, and the use of social sanction. Bearing babies irresponsibly is simply wrong. Failure to support children one has fathered is wrong. We must be unequivocal about this. It doesn't help matters when prime time TV has Murphy Brown, a character who supposedly epitomizes today's intelligent, highly-paid professional woman mocking the importance of a father by bearing a child alone and calling it just another lifestyle choice."

It is not fashionable to talk about moral values. Attack Hollywood and network television at the same time and they will fight back. They will fight back if we follow Dan Quayle's example, if we say that obedience to God's law will cure our social problems, if we say that following God's plan for marriage and the family will do more for people than welfare will.

It's time, Quayle said, to talk again about family, hard work, integrity, and personal responsibility. We cannot let ourselves be embarrassed out of our belief that two parents married to each other are in most cases better for children than is one parent; that honest work is better than handouts or crime; that we are brothers, and that we are our brothers' keepers; that it's worth making an effort, even when rewards aren't immediate.

Marriage is an area where the rewards aren't always immediate. That's an area where it's worth making an effort, if only, as Dan Quayle pointed out, because it tends to keep people out of poverty. Of course, earlier we looked at many other reasons for marriage, and why marriage is worthwhile, and why keeping marriages together is worthwhile.

If marriage is keeping people out of poverty, then divorce is plunging them into it. You undoubtedly know from your own experience people who have fallen into poverty because of divorce.

Let's see what the Word of God has to say about divorce. Malachi 2:16 tells us, " 'I hate divorce,' says the Lord God of Israel...So guard yourself in your spirit, and do not break faith."

There are Christians who have broken faith, broken their marriage vows, and there's no scriptural basis for it. They've sinned, and need to ask God for forgiveness. There's no other way to look at it.

On the other hand, there are some scriptural reasons for divorce. James 2:8-11 says:

If you really keep the royal law found in Scripture, "Love your neighbor as yourself," you are doing right. But if you show favoritism, you sin and are convicted by the law as lawbreakers. For whoever keeps the whole law and yet stumbles at just one point is guilty of breaking all of it. For He who said, "Do not commit adultery," also said, "Do not murder." If you do not commit adultery but do commit murder, you have become a lawbreaker (James 2:8-11).

A lot of people think they can divorce and still live holy lives. They think, "I know that God's Word didn't give me an out, but I took that out and I'm holding."

God says, "If you commit one sin, you're still a lawbreaker." God is a God of a second chance, but God is not a God of a second marriage.

In Matthew 19 Jesus talks about divorce.

Some Pharisees came to Him to test Him. They asked, "Is it lawful for a man to divorce his wife for any and every reason?"

"Haven't you read," He replied, "that at the beginning the Creator 'made them male and female,' and said, 'For this reason a man will leave his father and mother and be united to his wife, and the two will become one flesh'? So they are no longer two, but one. Therefore what God has joined together, let man not separate" (Matt. 19:3-6).

It's amazing how many people come to the house of God to get married but when they get in trouble, they go to secular counselors, and they go to the world to get separated. It's all God, God, God, when you want to come together. But when you want to get separated, it's man, man, man. Something's wrong with that, isn't there?

> *"...let man not separate."*
>
> *"Why then," they asked, "did Moses command that a man give his wife a certificate of divorce and send her away?"*
>
> *Jesus replied, "Moses permitted you to divorce your wives because your hearts were hard. But it was not this way from the beginning"* (Matt. 19:6-8).

In other words, divorce was not in God's original plan. When Adam and Eve got married, God didn't say, "Later on you can get a divorce." He intended Adam and Eve to be together forever.

Jesus spoke God's Word to them:

> *"I tell you that anyone who divorces his wife, except for marital unfaithfulness, and marries another woman commits adultery."*
>
> *The disciples said to him, "If this is the situation between a husband and wife, it is better not to marry."*
>
> *Jesus replied, "Not everyone can accept this word, but only those to whom it has been given"* (Matt. 19:9-11).

The Word of God has been given to us, and God expects us to accept His Word and live by it.

That's why I tell couples who want to get married, "You realize this is forever. Can you accept that? Are you ready to be with this person for the rest of your life?" Some people can't accept it.

Jesus told them, "Some are eunuchs because they were born that way; others were made that way by men; and others have renounced marriage because of the kingdom of heaven. The one who can accept this should accept it" (Matt. 19:12).

In other words, maybe God would like you to be single all your life, and there's nothing wrong with that. But if you say you want to get married, then you should be able to accept the Word of God and say that marriage is for life. And maybe the Apostles were right too: if you can't accept that, then it's better not to get married.

The Bible does give some reasons for divorce. The first is found in Matthew 5:27-28: "You have heard that it was said, 'Do not commit adultery.' But I tell you that anyone who looks at a woman lustfully has already committed adultery with her in his heart."

We can be unfaithful by giving our affections away to another person, and begin to love being around them more than we like our husband or wife. We can be unfaithful by giving someone else a tender touch that should belong only to our husband or wife. Even to look on another person and want him or her really bad is adultery.

"If your right eye causes you to sin, gouge it out and throw it away. It is better for you to lose one part of your body than for your whole body to be thrown into hell" (Matt. 5:29). If we followed that strictly, we would probably have a lot of people walking around with almost nothing left of their bodies.

"It has been said, 'Anyone who divorces his wife must give her a certificate of divorce.' But I tell you that anyone who divorces his wife, except for marital unfaithfulness, causes her to become an adulteress, and anyone who marries the divorced woman commits adultery" (Matt. 5:31-32).

One reason a person can get divorced is for adultery. Adultery is a spiritual death. Now, you can always forgive a person. It's hard to forgive for adultery, but it can be done. It takes a lot of strength. Now, what happens when a person commits adultery over and over again? It's going to be harder and harder to forgive, because something dies in the other person because the two of you have become one.

Let's look at First Corinthians 7:15-16: "But if the unbeliever leaves, let him do so. A believing man or woman is not bound in such circumstances; God has called us to live in peace. How do you know, wife, whether you will save your husband? Or how do you know, husband, whether you will save your wife?"

The point is this: if you are married to an unbeliever, and the person leaves, you do not have to follow. It's okay if you do: God has sanctified your household because of you. "For the unbelieving husband has been sanctified through his wife, and the unbelieving wife has been sanctified through her believing husband. Otherwise your children would be unclean, but as it is, they are holy" (1 Cor. 7:14).

Later in the same chapter we read, "A woman is bound to her husband as long as he lives. But if her husband dies, she is free to marry anyone she wishes, but he must belong to the Lord" (1 Cor. 7:39).

Finally, Malachi 2:14 (KJV) talks about dealing with your spouse treacherously. The New International Version calls it "broken faith." This comes right before the statement that God hates divorce. He warns us against dealing treacherously with our mate, and seems to equate that with divorce, with failure to keep the marriage covenant.

There's another kind of broken faith that can justify separation. If your husband molests your little girl, or is beating you, that is dealing treacherously. I could not in good conscience tell a wife to stay with such a husband, because he might just kill her. In that case, separation is a safety measure, and the wife still has an obligation to pray for her husband's salvation and healing.

God is going to hold us accountable. He's also going to hold you accountable for what you do. Because there are a lot of people who make decisions without getting any kind of counsel, and some people will receive counsel from anyone who agrees with them, so that they can do what they want to do. Even when a spouse does something treacherous, you should seek counsel about it.

Divorce, however, is not part of God's plan. I asked those people in my church who have been through divorce if they would comment on divorce, and tell the rest of us what the worst part of it is.

"Separation from your family," said one.

"Watching the pain the children go through."

"I was brought up in a pretty much dysfunctional family," one man said, "and growing up I had all kinds of crazy dreams about how I was going to get married and build a treehouse for my kids, and I developed strong family values...If we hadn't had any kids, it wouldn't have been so bad. But just watching all the dreams disappear...it still hurts..."

"When I divorced my husband," one woman said, "I still loved him, but it destroyed that love...the hardest part was the broken heart. Is this thing every going to heal?"

"Everybody thought we had an ideal marriage," one woman said. " 'They love each other. They're so sweet. They have fun.' We had no children. We had no real responsibility. We had a nice home, nice cars, we had money in the bank. We were married eight years. He just walked in one day and said, 'I no longer want to be married.' I really tried to get him to stay, but he wanted to go."

Here are some more comments from people:

"When my parents divorced, my idea of life was terrible. I couldn't trust anybody, because the trust was broken in the home. Even after I met the Lord, it was seven years before I was actually at the point of forgiveness for everything that was done."

"I couldn't understand because both of us were serving the Lord. We'd been married eighteen years, and I had been walking with the Lord twelve of those years. My husband had been walking seven years with the Lord, and I just couldn't understand. He decided to go back to the things of the world, and I kept telling him, 'Look at the blessings we have received.' I had been told when we had been married seven years that we would never have children because my husband couldn't father any children. And the Lord blessed me with a son. And after my son was born, He blessed us with a beautiful daughter.

"But I know now that the Lord is going to deal with my husband. He pressed for the divorce last year. But it just recently became final because I wouldn't let go. I kept saying, 'No, this is not of God.'

"But the Lord told me, 'You have to let go for Me to work with him.' So I'm trusting and I'm standing on the Word of the Lord, and I'm going to come out victorious. But it was devastating to my children. They're still going through hard times, but God is great."

"The hardest part about divorce was accepting it as a failure."

"The hardest part for me was the trust that was destroyed. Even though we were only married two years, we were together for five years, including the two years of marriage. Not so much that it destroyed just my trust, but my children's trust. It destroyed my commitment to my heavenly Father also. I had stood before Him and made a vow to love and honor and cherish that man for the rest of my life. God says, 'Do not make a vow unless you plan to keep it.' That destroyed me because I had nothing to do with the divorce. I wasn't able to keep my vow."

"One of the hardest parts for me was embarrassment. I couldn't talk to family. I couldn't talk to a pastor. I didn't know what to do. At one point I wanted to just commit suicide, but I had a son who was five years old. And I looked at him and I thought, 'Who would take care of him?' It surely wouldn't be my ex. So I went to God in prayer. I would not talk about it. I just went behind closed doors and I prayed. And then all of a sudden that burden was lifted."

"When you go through a divorce and you don't really want it, you tend to look at yourself and say, 'What did I do wrong?' I almost went crazy asking, 'What could I have done to change this or to prevent it?' I finally realized that I could only change myself; I'm only responsible for myself, and I can't control the other person, and that it takes two people to make the marriage, and to make it work."

"The pain you go through, the separation, was the hardest thing for me. When I married her, she was saved, and there was no problem there. When I went away last year, I came back after the summer, and she had found a boyfriend and everything. That's what hurt me the most.

And right now I have no desire to go back to her, because she is not the same woman I married; she doesn't have Christ in her life."

"I was here in San Antonio, and then I went to Korea, and when I was there, that's when my wife told me she wanted a divorce, and it was like I felt dead inside, just that moment, and all I could think of was getting back and seeing the children. There was deadness inside for over a year. But I was in Christ Jesus. That made the difference. Another thing that helped me was the brothers and sisters in the Lord in Korea who gave me support, people I just could talk to. That makes a difference."

After talking with these people and after prayer and study, I believe that the Lord showed me that there are several stages of divorce.

The first thing that seems to happen is a separation that comes about. The separation might be disagreement, moving from that to conflict. If you stay in conflict, it can bring about separation. If there is nothing to close the gap, then you can be separated while living together. You can be called husband and wife and not talking, not communicating. That first stage of separation is very dangerous.

The second stage is a mourning that comes about. You know that something's wrong. Now, there may be some cases where you do not know that something's wrong. Your husband just comes in and says, "I want a divorce."

In this mourning, some people get so unhappy that they begin to cry, "I just want out of this. I'm miserable. This is like being in hell."

If they can't rectify that, they move into divorce.

There is another stage of mourning after the divorce, You feel empty. You feel that something has died on the inside. You find yourself single again—married for eighteen years or twenty years and all of a sudden you are single again.

A lot of people get into a relationship with someone new immediately after the divorce, but first mourning needs to take place. They're empty. They don't know where they're going.

That brings us to the last stage. Before you can go into another relationship, you need to feel whole again. There needs to be a waiting period.

Instead of keeping their commitments, or even waiting after being divorced, or maybe dumped by a live-in "lover," people go from one relationship to another.

People are doing this because they see their needs not being met. Yes, we all have needs, but marriage is also about meeting your partner's needs. If you're only focusing on your own needs, you can always find some reason to be dissatisfied.

If we want to keep our marriages together, we need to learn to focus on our mate's needs and meet them.

Ephesians 5:31 tells us that a man will leave his father and mother and be united to his wife, and the two will become one flesh. This does not necessarily mean leaving them physically, but leaving the attachments you have. A lot of people, whenever they get in trouble, always call Mama or Daddy. They may not live in their parents' house, but they can't stand on their own two feet, they're always dependent on their parents. God says that when you get married, you're supposed to leave them. Once you are in the partnership of marriage, you're supposed to have your needs met by your spouse, not by your parents. I wouldn't want my daughter to marry a man who has to call Mom and Dad every five months, saying, "Get me out of this one. We need some more money. I tried to do all I could do. Can you help me?"

Verse 32 tells us, "This is a profound mystery—but I am talking about Christ and the church. However, each one of you also must love his wife as he loves himself, and the wife must respect her husband." A lot of women are in relationships where they don't respect their husbands.

What things cause a woman to lose respect for her husband? Here are some of the answers the women in my church gave me:

When a man can't make a decision. There's nothing wrong with going to your wife for help, because that's what she's there for. But when a man won't make decisions, that can cause a woman to lose respect for him.

When a man will not provide for his family, his wife will lose respect for him.

A man who allows his wife to talk to him disrespectfully. Men talking about their wives in front of other men. A man who won't work. A man who treats other women more kindly than he treats his own wife. A man who doesn't know where he's going. A man who insults his wife. A man whose word doesn't mean anything. A man who will not discipline his children. All these things can cause a wife to lose respect for her husband.

Every man needs to be on guard against these problems in himself; if he fails to meet his wife's needs, she will be tempted to look somewhere else. Every woman needs to be looking to meet her husband's needs.

Otherwise we will be calling it quits when we're under attack. The enemy loves to have us fighting each other instead of fighting him.

Reflections

1. It's amazing how many people come to the house of God to get married; but when they get in trouble, they go to secular counselors, and they go to the world to get separated.

2. If you're only focusing on your own needs, you can always find some reason to be dissatisfied.

3. The enemy loves to have us fighting each other, instead of fighting him.

Chapter 7

Sources of Problems

Ephesians 5 tells us that the husband must love his wife, and that the wife must respect her husband.

What would cause a man not to love his wife? I asked my congregation this. Here are some of their answers:

Nagging. Lack of respect from his wife. Lies. His wife doesn't listen to him. She gives more affection and time to others than to him. A wife who won't communicate. A wife who doesn't respect herself. An untidy wife. A sneaky wife. A wife who competes with her husband. A wife who won't boost his ego. Being treated like a child. A wife who is very moody and always crying. A wife who is contradictory and argumentative. A wife who manipulates. A wife who is critical and untrustworthy. A wife who talks down to her husband.

All these things are examples of needs not being met. This is not to say that a man has an excuse not to love his wife just because she's not perfect. Nobody's perfect, and anyway we husbands are *commanded* to love our wives. But a man does have a need for certain things from his wife, and not every husband is mature enough to keep loving his wife if she's not meeting his needs. So unmet needs can still be a problem, because none of us is perfect.

We can learn something about needs from Abraham Maslow. He was a great psychologist. He came up with a hierarchy of needs.

Abraham Maslow, an American psychologist said that our basic needs are physiological: food, water, shelter, even sex can be a physiological need.

Next are needs for safety and security: job security, financial security, a feeling of safety in your home, freedom from bodily harm. However, these needs are not as elementary as the physiological needs. People who lack food and water will disregard safety in order to get food and water. If you get hungry enough, you care about food more than about feeling secure.

The next need is for acceptance: things like friendship, belonging, love, esteem, achievement. Again, in the hierarchy, you don't worry much about feeling accepted if you don't have anything to eat. If you're hungry enough, you'll eat out of a garbage can even if it's not socially acceptable.

Finally you have a need for what he called self-actualization, being able to reach your potential, that you can become the person you want to be.

And some schools of thought say that people often want to have achievement and job satisfaction and status and friendship even more than they want the physiological needs. Some people will even kill themselves over a lost friendship or broken relationship. You will find people who are down and out, homeless, because when their social needs weren't met, they didn't have the psychological strength left to look after their own more basic needs. But the needs are still there.

In marriage, you can see that happening. When disaster strikes, and you're in a life-and-death situation, often a husband-and-wife team will pull together beautifully. But when things settle down and the emergency is over, sometimes the same couple will be at odds with each other. Their basic needs are met, and now they're looking at higher things like companionship and where they're going in life, things that maybe the other person isn't equipped to provide. When you get married, it's difficult for one person to meet all these needs, and a lot of things go wrong in marriage because people find their needs not being met.

Here's an important lesson for married couples: Jesus Christ meets all these needs. If I belong to the Body of Christ, I'm part of the biggest family in the world. Christ provides self-esteem. He says I'm more than a conqueror. Self-actualization? I can be all that I can be in Christ Jesus. And I can do anything through Christ Jesus, Who strengthens me. A person who does not know Jesus Christ is out on a limb because he or she will be expecting the spouse to be everything.

We looked at levels of needs. Jesus Christ is on a much higher level. Let's look at First Corinthians 7:32-35.

> *I would like you to be free from concern. An unmarried man is concerned about the Lord's affairs—how he can please the Lord. But a married man is concerned about the affairs of this world—how he can please his wife—and his interests are divided. An unmarried woman or virgin is concerned about the Lord's affairs: Her aim is to be devoted to the Lord in both body and spirit. But a married woman is concerned about the affairs of this world—how she can please her husband. I'm saying this for your own good, not to restrict you, but that you may live in a right way in undivided devotion to the Lord* (1 Cor. 7:32-35).

When people get married, even though the Lord has been meeting all their needs, sometimes they no longer want the Lord to meet these needs. Because the two have become one flesh, they start looking directly to each other. There is no way that your spouse is going to meet all your needs.

But even though the Lord does look after us and provides everything we need, He commonly works through other people. We should be looking to meet each other's needs, without putting an impossible burden on each other.

How do we keep aware of each other's needs? Sensitivity. Bible study—yes, the Bible shows us how to serve each other. Communication. When you communicate, you have to have the right attitude: an attitude that's not self-seeking.

But there are needs that we ourselves aren't aware of, and we can't always communicate them. Even after being married many years, there are still things about my wife that I don't know.

How do you discover the unknown needs? Sometimes you get to a moment of truth when you get that person to open up—not by asking, "What do you want?" Not by demanding, "Why don't you tell me what you need?"

There are always signs, and when you begin to see those signs, you begin to tune in and think. Time brings about changes, age brings about changes, and we have to grow together in order to know who each other is. But, when we believe that we know everything about our mate, our mate will eventually become boring to us and its easy to become attracted to someone else. We need to learn how to be there for each other. How do we do this?

Matthew 23:11-12 gives us the answer:

> *The greatest among you will be your servant. For whoever exalts himself will be humbled, and whoever humbles himself will be exalted* (Matt. 23:11-12).

In marriage, when you acquire the attitude of being a servant, you will become aware of the other person's needs.

What is a servant? Picture a waitress. She stands there and asks, "Do you need some more food? Or do you need your glass filled?" The disciples knew what Jesus was talking about. That's why they were shocked when He started to wash their feet. Are we ready to do that for our husbands and wives? It's just like serving food. You see something getting empty, and you respond to that. You learn how to minister to one another. You learn how to fill the need of the moment. You also learn how to give understanding to each other.

Some people are selfish. They don't want to serve anyone. They think, "I'm not going to be your servant. Do you think I'm going to wait on you?" Yes, that's what God wants. That's what He did for us. That's what He wants us to do for each other. That's what He's going to do for us at the heavenly banquet. It's time we got in step with the Kingdom of Heaven, which is made up of servants.

Lastly, we learn to become aware of our responsibility to fill each other's needs. A waiter or waitress doesn't just hang around the restaurant and give you service when it's convenient. No, giving you service is the servant's job. It's an obligation if you want to work in a restaurant. It's an obligation if you want to work at a marriage.

In marriage, it should be mutual giving and mutual serving. The husband should have the same kind of servant's attitude as his wife has. But in a lot of relationships, there isn't mutual giving. We think of husband and wife sharing the load 50/50. Sometimes it may be 80/20, and the person who's giving 80% finds that it starts to wear on him or her. If you're always the one to apologize, eventually this thing will bother you.

Sometimes there might be relationships that are 100/0. Somebody's always giving. The other person is like a doorknob. Like a brick wall. An argument comes up, and that person will never apologize. Let's remember that Christ gave 100% when we were still giving nothing. But because we're human, it is very difficult to be the one doing all the giving. Longsuffering doesn't mean "always" with God. Many times in the Bible God got upset. He said, "Look, I've had enough." God told the children of Israel, "You're My people, and I love you." But there were times in the Bible when God was getting ready to kill all of them. What's going on in this world right now is eventually going to come to an end. There are a lot of people who are legally married, and that's it. There is no relationship there at all. There is no initiative to meet any needs, because they have brought about a separation in the relationship. There are people who are doing things right now, thinking they're getting away with it. There is no getting away with anything. It's going to end, and there will be justice.

But if both husband and wife have the servant's attitude, one is going to give and be there for the other; both win. If we're one flesh, then when you win, I win.

Besides meeting each other's needs, we should be looking out for each other's wants. Now, a need is something you have to have; a want is something you desire. Needs are more important than wants, but we should be looking out for each other's wants if only because it's what we're always asking of God. It's true; let's admit it. How many of the things we ask God for are things we absolutely have to have?

But if we are putting God and His Kingdom first, He is pleased to give us our desires too. We should try not only to see that each other's needs are met, but to please each other.

Now, a need is not always obvious. It could be something that is necessary to keep the relationship alive and vibrant. The relationship could be dead, and need to be resurrected. Some husbands and wives are so miserable, just living together. They might even sleep in the same bed. They might sit at the same table and eat dinner, but they are strangers. They haven't been looking out for each other's needs, much less trying to please each other.

When needs go unmet, a person will become a prime candidate to be tempted by the devil to have an affair, or to give affection to someone else. This is especially dangerous because most people don't even know how to meet each other's needs, because they never have identified them, and probably have never even talked about things like this. Even a lot of Christian marriages have this trouble, because they forget that we're in the flesh.

People don't want to talk about certain things in the church. Sex is one. Marital relationships are another. Disciplining children is another. Money is another. I'm tired of seeing relationships break up because of the example of the man of God in the pulpit, who has been married three or four times. Or by people who say they love the Lord but get married every five years. I would rather talk about it and prevent problems from happening. People might be having problems in their sexual relationship and be embarrassed to come to a man of God or woman of God and talk about it. They get divorced, yet if they had come and talked to someone about it, possibly their marriage would have been saved.

But God has called us to something more. He's given us His plan for loving each other, and if we follow it we won't have to worry about our partner being tempted by the devil. God can give us an affair-proof relationship.

But we need His help. It doesn't matter how spiritual you are, how much you speak in tongues, how much you worship, or even how much you pray. When you mesh two personalities together, there's nothing like it in the world. It's a mystery. And we need all the help we can get. And we need to base our relationship on the Word of God.

To live our calling as husbands and wives, father and mothers, we need incredible strength. But when we're weak, He's strong. Then, although we are weak, we have His strength in us. Incredible strength, that's what God has given us. When you think you can't go anymore, you will have His strength.

Like the bones in the valley having life restored to them, we, by learning how to meet each other's needs, can rebuild a marriage. Remember that our greatest need is our need for God. When a relationship isn't functioning any more, you still have Jesus Christ. You can fall back and say, "It's in Him that I live and move and have my being."

God provides. Psalm 104:27-30 tells us:

> *These all look to You to give them their food at the proper time. When You give it to them, they gather it up; when You open Your hand, they are satisfied with good things. When You hide Your face, they are terrified; when You take away their breath, they die and return to the dust. When You send Your Spirit, they are created, and You renew the face of the earth* (Ps. 104:27-30).

That's what God's power does in us. It renews us. If we are willing to cooperate and obey, we will be renewed and recreated. Our relationship will be renewed and recreated.

Reflections

1. A person who does not know Jesus Christ is out on a limb because he or she will be expecting the spouse to be everything.

2. When needs are not met, a person will become a prime candidate to be tempted by the devil to have an affair or to give affection to someone else.

3. When a relationship isn't functioning anymore, you still have Jesus Christ.

Chapter 8

The Need for Discipline

What are the duties of parents, according to the Word of God? Let's look at Deuteronomy 6:5-9.

> *Love the Lord your God with all your heart and with all your soul and with all your strength. These commandments that I give you today are to be upon your hearts. Impress them on your children. Talk about them when you sit at home and when you walk along the road, when you lie down and when you get up. Tie them as symbols on your hands and bind them on your foreheads. Write them on the doorframes of your houses and on your gates* (Deut. 6:5-9).

We need to talk of God's commandments to our children. We need to be teaching them by word and by example at all times. This needs to be a way of life. The pressure from the outside is so great now that those who are not living by this Word will fall. There's going to be a fall; there's even going to be a falling away.

There are things that we've been doing and our parents have been doing; we can't stop doing these things now: praying over our food, praying over our children, anointing them with oil, telling them about Jesus, telling them that Jesus is the only way. Even if the world goes by what's on television and tells you there's more than one way, and regardless of what the colleges and universities are saying, we still need to tell our children that there's only one way. Even if the world says we're closed-minded, Jesus is the only way.

Some churches are becoming afraid to preach and teach the truth because of what's coming. Just look around. The Word says that Jesus was born of a virgin. If God's Word says it happened, it happened. He rose on the third day. He was dead and He arose.

> *Do what is right and good in the Lord's sight, so that it may go well with you and you may go in and take over the land that the Lord promised on oath to your forefathers, thrusting out all your enemies before you…* (Deut. 6:18).

Do what is right and good in the Lord's sight, so that it may go well with you. Doing what is right doesn't mean parents are supposed to be Mr. Nice Guy.

Parents don't need to be brothers or sisters to their children. It's okay to be friends, but don't be just good friends—be parents.

Many children today have bad manners. (We have good children too.) But one thing that really bothers me is to see parents look the other way when their children display bad manners. This is contempt for authority. It's so widespread, it's unbelievable. It's complete disrespect. And it is not just that the children have contempt for authority, but that the parents have no respect for their own God-given authority.

I was in the mall and saw a little boy's father tell him to stop doing something; the boy started kicking his father. As I was walking by, I said, "Lord, help me, God." I've never before seen so many children and young people who don't like to work. Never before have I seen grown men lie in their beds till noon while their mothers and fathers have to beg them to get up and go and look for a job.

Why do we have the kind of parents we have today? Here are some comments from the people in my church:

Parents are afraid of their children.

Daddy's missing.

Mothers are often raising their children with live-in boyfriends.

Being too liberal with the children, giving them free rein. They can go and come whenever they want.

The independence that this world is teaching kids.

Parents are too busy doing their own thing.

A younger generation has had children, but they're not responsible.

People see children not as God gave them, as a blessing, but as interference with their lives.

The shows on television where the majority of the people always go along with the wrong way, the way against God. They will applaud whatever makes people happy.

With the lack of biblical foundation, immorality rises, and a lot of the parents have abandoned their morals.

In 1960, the greatest influence on children was parents; church was second, then other areas. But in 1990, the number-one influence on children was media.

Teenagers are having babies and no one is giving them proper guidance on how to raise children. So when they get older, they want to become friends with their children, because they never really had any friends when they were trying to raise the children.

If they had parents who were hard on them, they turn around and are lenient with their children.

Children are raising themselves, because our society has pulled the mothers away from the home front, and television is raising our children; other people are raising our children. The world has given us substitutes for parents.

Discipline is missing.

That last one sums it up well. It's missing in families, and it's missing in education. A lot of people feel that the qualification of the teacher is the most important thing. Being able to love the children when you're teaching them is just as important. When I was in school, I had teachers who would spank me if I did something wrong, and then they would tell my parents. The teachers and parents were all part of the community. Now, in a lot of communities, parents don't know the teachers. And some of the teachers really don't care about those children. These problems are reasons why so many churches are building their own schools.

Since we often can't rely on the schools to provide discipline any more, the burden falls even heavier in the home. Single parents are sometimes caught in the middle.

Single parents are now heading a very large proportion of America's families and, as Dan Quayle pointed out in his much-talked-about speech,* these are the families most likely to be in poverty. Many people don't realize, however, that single fathers make up an increasingly large number of the single parents heading households. Most of their situations are not like Mr. Mom's. *Newsweek* reported that "Single fathers are now one of the fastest growing segments of the American population.... The increase in single fathers was as inevitable as kids outgrowing their sneakers. Many men who have come to take

* May 20, 1992.

an active role in bringing up their children simply aren't willing to give them up when a marriage or relationship dissolves. Traditionally, mothers were almost automatically awarded custody of a couple's children, especially very young ones. But now judges place more emphasis on the best interests of the child and, with fewer moms staying home full time these days, those interests aren't nearly so clear cut as they once were.... Single fatherhood imposes big changes on a man's life."* The article mention a thirty-three-year-old man from Quincy, Massachusetts, whose wife left him in 1991 with two young sons. He'd been working staggered shifts, and couldn't afford daycare that would be available round the clock. So he quit work and went on welfare to take care of his kids.

"Single fathers," the article continued, "can also face judicial and professional discrimination. Some contend that courts remain biased against them." One man said he felt he had to prove he could be a mother.

Even though single parenting is something that we have to live with, and single parents often do a very, very good job, it's very difficult for a man to raise his little girls to grow up to be women. There are certain things that only women can do. There are certain things that only men can do. A woman can't teach a man how to be a man.

The problem of single parents boils down to this: they are working with only half a husband-and-wife team.

---

* *Newsweek*, December 14, 1992.

One woman in our church said to me, "Pastor, I am a single parent. I have children, teenagers, and to a certain extent, they are raising themselves, because I have to have two jobs right now."

There's one thing she should be applauded for. She's sitting in church, and one of her daughters is with her. In cases like that, the responsibility falls on the young people in a different way too. The youth have an awesome responsibility. Their parents are not always able to give them the kind of parenting a lot of us older folks received as kids. Nowadays the parents are more apt to be single, or just ill prepared for parenting. Some of us need to learn how to be parents. Parenting is a learned skill. One is not born with this skill, it is a learned behavior. It comes from learning, trial and error, observation and practice.

Parents need to be the example for their children. Children need order. I asked the young people in our church about the discipline they receive from their parents. "Why would you want to go to the limit?" I asked them.

"I would provoke my father," one young man answered. "I would see just how far I could go, but I wanted to see if he disciplined me because he loved me. Because I figured if he didn't do anything to me, I didn't think he cared."

"Kids push their parents to the limit," another said, "because they're spoiled and they know if they push them to the limit, they'll get what they want."

"Pastor," another said, "at five, I was a child who was full of foolishness. I would do anything for excitement. I remember I stole one time. I stole a lady's baby that was three days old because she wouldn't let me hold the baby, and so when she went to wash her clothes, I went into the house and got the baby and took the baby out of the house."

"I think about all those things I did as a child, and reading in the Bible where it says foolishness is bound in the heart of a child. I can think of those times when, you know, if my grandmother had not stopped me then, I would be in some penitentiary today. I would probably go steal an airplane just for excitement today. But I praise God that the thought of somebody stealing something now makes me nervous."

It's not being mean when you discipline your children. You're doing what the Lord has told you to do. And it's only for a season. I had strict discipline as a child, but don't look at me and feel sorry for me. I had a happy childhood. We laughed, we talked, we played, we had more than anybody on the street. But I got corrected.

But living by the Bible, particularly in the area of raising children, is getting more and more difficult. The Bible says that certain things are right and certain things are wrong, and that makes wrongdoers uncomfortable.

Because the Bible *does* condemn sin, it's getting very unpopular to believe what the Bible says. It's becoming very unpopular for us to say that sex outside of marriage is wrong, to say that homosexuality is wrong, and to talk against abortion.

This last presidential election, in my estimation, was the people's choice. It was "Give us Barrabas. I don't want morality. Barrabas is going to give us economic wealth." A lot of Christians are going to go in the closet, because they're going to be afraid. In your life outside the home—at work, at school, even at church—do not be ashamed to live by the Bible. At home, do not be ashamed to live by the Bible. Be not afraid.

I see things that make me want to be afraid. I watched a television program the other night that really disturbed me. It showed a videotape of several public school classrooms. It was complete chaos. Chaos! The children were throwing things. They were fighting. They were spinning around the classroom, turning their chairs over while the teacher was trying to teach. The tape showed several other classooms, where the same thing was going on. And this is going on all over the nation. Teachers are quitting in droves, because they don't want to put up with the violence in the schools, because they can't even teach the children, who can't sit down and keep still.

Then they took the video and showed it to the parents, who were in shock that their children acted the way they did. Some of the parents blamed the teachers. When children show contempt for authority, disrespect for people, and won't work, this is not just the fault of the schools. In fact, if the parents aren't doing their job, it's almost impossible for even the best schools to overcome that.

One day-care provider wrote that she was puzzled by unruly kids. "I am a mother of two young children, and I provide family care in my home," she wrote. "I am amazed at the enormous amount of disrespectful children I have encountered. I have seen kids kick, slap, and yell at their parents. Yet nothing but an empty threat is made. It's bad enough when parents see their child kicking or slapping another child. But when the parent is the one getting abused, I believe that it's time for immediate discipline. Unfortunately, very few parents do anything at all."

We are in this awful situation because the parents themselves have rebelled against authority, and now they're raising children who disrespect authority too. Many parents don't know how to impose discipline because they never learned discipline themselves. And many parents are too inconsistent when it comes to discipline. A lot of parents make up rules on the spot. Or they make idle threats. We need to say what we mean and mean what we say. But a lot of us won't take the time and trouble to discipline our kids. It's hard work. One of the parents on the program said that as a single parent she didn't have time to raise her kids properly. If we don't have time for one of our most important responsibilities—raising our children—then our priorities are completely out of order.

We often have problems with children when most of the discipline is left up to the mother. Our liberal society tells us that children should be manipulated and tricked into obedience rather than doing what we tell them to do. Most fathers will say, "Do what I tell you now."

When I went through school, my mother and father knew the teachers, and if I did something wrong, the teacher would correct me, and also tell my parents.

The father is supposed to maintain discipline. Sometimes there's a problem because the father is strict only in certain situations. He might be strict about grades in school, but lax about church attendance, enforcing the rules only in those areas that are important to him.

Parents need to enforce discipline; they also need to set the example. You know, children are very smart. They sense the spirit that is coming from you. If I tell my children, "No," I mean it, and I've thought the thing through. Many children actually boss their parents around. I've seen children who actually strike their parents. Discipline is totally lacking.

Why do many children continue to misbehave after you punish them? Most children know how far they can push their parents. When a parent says, "Stop doing that," and then starts counting, that's hurting the children. It's teaching them that they don't have to obey the first time they're told.

Make sure the punishment is consistent and unpleasant. Some kinds of behavior, it seems, can only be driven out by spanking. Children who lie and steal, and hurt other children, you have to spank them. You don't say, "No, no. Now, let me just explain to you that you don't steal." There must be punishment.

My children will tell you that I am a stickler for character things. If I see that they tend to lie or cheat, I go berserk. And I can't stand to see them fighting among themselves.

If a child steals, chances are that the first time you catch him is not the first time he's done it. Make the child take it back and face the person it was stolen from. This has a powerful effect. They would rather die than be publicly exposed. If they've stolen candy from a store, make them go back, even if they've eaten the candy, and talk to the manager, who will help you to put fear into them. Let them see the police if need be. Let them see everything they need to see. But most people are so busy trying to protect their children that they neglect discipline.

What about timing? The optimum thing to do is to punish the child immediately. But there are times when the child knows that you don't want to make a scene. If you are inconsistent with punishing disobedience, that child will take advantage of the situation every time. But if your child knows that you mean what you say and say what you mean, you can say, "You'll be punished when we get home. They can bank on it. But if the child knows that by the time you get home, you're going to forget about it, then you're going to have the child taking advantage of you.

How can you let your children know you mean what you say?

1. *Be consistent.*

2. *Make your expectations clear.* Let there be no doubt in their minds what your expectations are. It bothers me when my children come to me and say, "I thought you meant this," and they are lying. I spank them just for telling me that.

3. *Discuss your rules.* I used to break my father's rules sometimes because of peer pressure, and I had to suffer the consequences. If my father said, "Be in the house at one o'clock in the morning," and I came in at 1:15, I wouldn't get into the house.

4. *Don't make everything a major issue.* If everything is a major issue, then you put the children on the defensive. Certain things are more important than others.

5. *Don't play favorites.* I love all three of my children. I believe I love them equally. I don't play favorites. What goes for Eric goes for Erica, and what goes for Erica goes for Elisha. Don't play favorites. Children know when you play favorites.

6. *Don't use one child as a scapegoat to get your point across.* You know, people even do that in church, or on the job. Deal with the person who is causing the problem.

7. *Don't make promises you can't keep.*

8. *Don't be too critical.* A lot of parents today, because they can't discipline their children, tell them, "You'll never be anything." You're putting that in their spirit.

9. *Don't criticize and praise at the same time when you discipline.* If somebody has done something wrong, then tell them.

Good discipline reinforces your family goals and values. Good discipline builds self-control in the child. A lot of children even now, sixteen, seventeen years old, don't have any self-control at all. And discipline helps to build self-control, especially at an early age.

Discipline is the first step in helping our children to grow up. But it extends to more areas than punishment. We have to help them learn to take responsibility for their own actions, and teach them not to dodge responsibility. Try not to rescue them every time they make a mistake. Sometimes it's good when our children make mistakes; we can talk to them about it, see if they learned anything from what they did. Also, when they make a mistake, they can identify with it: "This is my mistake. I did this." But parents must know the limits that children have. That comes through communication. If they make a major mistake, you must know their limits, and see where they are, so they won't get hurt. You have to coach them along.

When children don't learn from their mistakes, they think there's nothing wrong with it. They expect their parents to come to their rescue every time.

When I took Eric to school in San Diego and it was time for us to leave, it was very difficult. It crushed Eric. But we had to go. "We have to go get on the plane," I said, and I hugged him.

He was standing on the corner, tears coming down his face, and Erica cried, "Dad, how could you do that to your own son!"

I said to Eric, "I can't do it for you. Your mama can't do it for you. You're going to have to do this for yourself."

When I got home, I told my wife what had happened. Erica said, "Mom, Dad just drove off!"

My wife asked, "Honey, how did you do it? I know I should have gone." She was going to pull him out of school.

"Honey," I said, "you can't pull him out of school. He's going to have to go through this thing for himself." When parents see their children go through things, they want to go in there and rescue them, and make them comfortable. That's not going to help them grow. We have to learn to let them go.

That was not a situation where my son was not permitted to stay home any longer. It was just time for him to learn to be on his own. But some of you need to kick your kids out of the house. If you have a twenty-eight-year-old guy lying around at home, when he's forty-two years old, he'll be saying, "Mama, do you have dinner ready yet?"

I'm not talking about discipline where you go and hurt somebody. I'm talking about discipline in love.

"Many parents of this generation cannot separate discipline from abuse," one woman in my congregation told me. "Every time you spank a child, it doesn't mean you're abusing that child, but only you know that. Most of the time when children are abused it's because they've gotten away with so much that they make you angry till you beat them."

Fathers, if your children don't respond to your wife's voice, you can help your wife out. Let them know that the next time their mother tells them something, they'd better do it. You are reinforcing the mother.

In the partnership of marriage, especially in the way we relate to and discipline our children, we need to be together. We have to work towards unity between husband and wife, and then that unity will be something we can share in a different way with our children: we will teach them to be one with each other as brothers and sisters, and one with God.

Reflections

1. Children are raising themselves because our society has pulled the mothers away from the home front.

2. The world has given us substitutes for parents.

3. Good discipline reinforces your family goals and values.

4. Good discipline builds self-control in the child.

5. Discipline is the first step in helping our children to grow up.

Chapter 9

Resolving Differences and Conflicts

A recent newspaper report* said that half of all couples are unhappy. A study indicated that about twenty-three percent of couples have really good marriages, and another twenty-five percent could have good ones if they took some kind of marriage enrichment course. These estimates come from University of Minnesota researcher David Olson. But fifty percent, unless they get genuine professional therapy, probably will never be happy, he says. Olson, who spoke recently at the conference of the

* *San Antonio Light* from *USA Today*

American Association for Marriage and Family Therapy, bases his estimates on research with more than 15,300 couples.

He also indicated some factors that predict happiness for marriages: good communication skills and the ability to solve conflicts constructively; personality compatibility; agreement on religious values; and the quality of sex life, among other things.

Another article, in the *San Antonio Light,*[*] stated that the sexes struggle to communicate different needs, that men and women need to understand that there is a difference between men and women. It said that without the awareness that we are supposed to be different, men and women are at odds with each. We usually become angry or frustrated with the opposite sex because we have forgotten this important truth. We expect the opposite sex to be more like ourselves. We desire them to want what we want and to feel the way we feel.

Men and women communicate differently, yet another article tells us. "For women, communication is of primary importance."

Another article was entitled "Mastering the Uncommon Art of Communication."[**] "Are you a great communicator?" it asked. "If you're married, you'd better become one, because nothing has a greater impact on your marriage than your ability to communicate effectively with

* John Gray *San Antonio Light*, Nov. 4, 1992.

** Mac Hammond, *Believer's Voice of Victory*

your spouse. If you don't communicate well, your marriage is not going to be everything God intended it to be."

"Communication is so important," this article stated, "that God named Jesus...the living Word...God's communication to mankind....Just as God communicates to us through Jesus, we should communicate Jesus to one another. Everything you say to your spouse should in some way reveal the character of Jesus."

This article tells us to "Offend not! The first and most important key to effective communication is: Avoid Offending Your Listener....Defensiveness distorts the listener's interpretation of your words....Be swift to hear....Listening has a powerfully positive impact on your partner. More than anything else you can do or say, listening demonstrates that you care. Listening says, 'Your feelings are important to me.' "

It goes on, "Dare to admit you're wrong. All of us like to think we're right."

Communication is a key not only to preserving and building relationships, but to restoring broken ones. "You can learn to resolve conflict," another article said "but only if you recognize the need for the presence of the living God, Who helps us heal from the inside out."

Communication brings couples together, brings families together.

One problem we have with communication is that we always want to express what's on our minds *right now.* When something's bothering us, we tend to focus on only that. To help overcome that problem, I've come up with a suggestion for married couples:

When your relationship is at its peak of happiness, make a written list of good qualities and things you like about your mate. Put this list in a sealed envelope, and put the envelope in a secret place where only you can find it.

When you have a bad argument or a serious conflict in your marriage, go and get the envelope, open it and read it. What you wrote on the list will help you regain focus and help you take the first step toward wanting to forgive.

Healing in the process of forgiveness is usually gradual. Forgiveness doesn't mean the pain will go away immediately. But you must continue to function in your marriage even when it hurts, because the devil would rather have you keep track of wrongs and stew about them. If you stockpile your emotions until you explode, you could bring a fatal wound to your relationship. Don't hold things in. Don't keep a record of wrongs.

What we keep a record of contributes greatly to the picture we have of each other. If we're always thinking about how we've been wronged, we're going to have a negative picture of our mate.

On the other hand, if we keep looking for and acknowledging and praising the good things, we'll have a more positive picture of each other. We'll be better able to see the other person as God sees him or her. We'll be able to see God in the other person. That's important.

Fathers represent God to the family. And the fathers are primarily responsible to ensure that the children receive training in the Lord. Just as Jesus is God's Word to us, fathers represent God to the family. Of course, none of us human fathers is a perfect image of God the Father. Jesus is. So it's important not only to teach our children by example, but to introduce them to Jesus. But when children are small, example is much stronger than words, and their impression of God is usually formed by their fathers. If the father is a strict disciplinarian, children assume that God's that way.

Ephesians 6:4 tells us, *"Fathers do not exasperate your children; instead, bring them up in the training and instruction of the Lord."* Fathers must maintain firm discipline, but at the same time maintain regular communication. A lot of children identify mostly with their mother because the father never communicates with them.

The father is to give instruction and the mother is to give teaching. There's a difference between instruction and teaching. Giving instruction could mean telling a child, "I want you to get your books out and study." Instructions might give a course of direction, or a plan. Teaching goes on all the time. But the mothers are usually with the children more than the fathers, simply because our society has it structured that much of the father's time is spent away from home. Often, *both* of them are out working.

Proverbs 1:8 says, *"Listen, my son, to your father's instruction and do not forsake your mother's teaching."* A mother should always be giving her children lessons. The father needs to give instruction, direction and orders, primarily, but should also be there to communicate with the children. You want your children not only to come to their mother, but to be able to come to the father too. A lot of children don't come to their fathers because the only time their fathers talk to them is when they are spanking them or disciplining them.

The father is supposed to make sure that firm discipline is maintained in the home. It has to be maintained by him. There is no appeal beyond the father. When he walks through the home, he'll say, "All right, lights out now. I heard your mother tell you to put the lights out. Lights will be turned out right now." The father backs up the mother and enforces what she says.

The mother is supposed to give consistent, loving discipline, firm correction, so that the children can learn to discipline themselves. That's what teaching is all about.

Proverbs 29:15 states, *"The rod of correction imparts wisdom, but a child left to himself disgraces his mother."* When a child is unruly, that disgrace falls on both the parents, but primarily on the mother.

As one man at our church pointed out, only when a child knows that the mother is serious will he obey. Too many mothers say, "Wait till your dad gets home." It's a weak woman who says that, and it makes the child look at his father as just an authoritarian. But when the child knows that his mother doesn't need her husband to make the child behave, knows that order will be established in the home without waiting for the father to get home, he will act right.

When something goes wrong, there needs to be some spanking, some correction, some discipline right there on the spot.

The family needs to be a classroom for instruction for the children, and the parents ought to be the primary teachers, not the television, and not the teachers at school.

In Ephesians 6:1-2 we find two commands for children. The first is: *"Children, obey your parents in the Lord, for this is right."* The second command is: *"Honor your father and mother."*

"Obey" means to do what your parents say while you're living with them. "Honor" means to love and respect them for the rest of your life. There's a difference there. I honor my mother and father right now. I'm almost 45 years old, and I still honor them, and I even obey them—sometimes. But I have already left my father and mother, and I cleave to my wife now. As long as I lived with them, I was to obey them. I must honor them and give them respect as long as I live.

It doesn't matter how educated you get, how much money you have. It doesn't matter what city you live in. Some people move out of the country and come to the city, and look down on their parents now because their parents do not seem as sophisticated as they are.

It doesn't matter what kind of position you've achieved. When my father comes to our church, I honor him.

One member of our church brought up another side to the issue:

Children who have step-parents sometimes try to excuse disobedience by saying, "I don't have to listen to him, because he's not my real dad." If you're living with this person, and he's supplying everything you need, then you need to respect and obey him. Your real daddy may not even be sending child support. You know what I'm saying? But this is your parent. Your real mother may be someplace else, and this woman is doing all she can to be a parent for you. You honor your mother and your father, step-parents and natural parents.

Don't be afraid of this Word. You have to learn how to embrace it. What's right is right; truth is truth. Some people don't want to hear the Word because they want an excuse to do what they want to do.

Another issue that stems from this verse in Ephesians 6:1: The Bible says, "*Children, obey your parents in the Lord.*" If a parent is unsaved, if he's telling them what is right, the children still have to obey him.

When you are older, and make more decisions on your own, there may be times when, as a matter of conscience, you do have to refuse your parents. Your father wants you to get drunk with him? You have to say, "Dad, I'm sorry, I can't do that. I'm a Christian. I've dedicated my life to the Lord."

That doesn't mean children should ever stop honoring their parents. Ephesians 6:2-3 says, " *'Honor your father and mother'—which is the first commandment with a promise—'that it may go well with you and that you may enjoy long life on the earth.'* " We have a commandment with a blessing.

Now, those who are not honoring their parents will not have long life. Things will not go well with you. You will not be blessed. What goes around comes around. You think you might be getting away with something. No, you're just getting by.

What about children who have been abused by their parents, who have been molested by their parents? The Word says to honor our parents. I've heard people say, "I can't respect my parents because they did such things to me." How can those children find hope in this Word?

After you become a Christian, there is nothing a person can do to you that you shouldn't at least try to forgive. When we learn to forgive, we also are set free from the thing that was done to us. First we have to forgive; then we have to ask God to help us obey His Word.

God judges us by our heart. He doesn't look just at the outward appearance. He knows what we're trying to do. It's difficult to forgive someone for something like that. I won't say it's easy, and when you forgive, the hurt doesn't go away either. Being a Christian, you still have to walk in that principle of forgiveness, even forgiving child abuse. If you're not able to yet, you have to ask God to help you get there, so that you can honor your parents.

What if your parents have changed? Some parents have abused their children, and now they've truly seen the light. That does not make it right, but they are sorry for what they did. They were blinded by satan. And some of them may be even saved right now.

There are things, even in my life and your life, that we've done and for which God has forgiven us. No sin is beyond forgiveness, even murder.

Obedience is the highest form of worship, and to forgive and honor your parents is to obey God. Until you reach that point of starting to forgive, no healing can take place. The hurt is still there. The anger and resentment are still there. Once you forgive, you're not saying that what happened was okay; you forgive in order to go through a healing process, not so much that you relieve them of responsibility. You have to have some kind of settlement with yourself.

There are so many women and men, but mostly women, who have been sexually abused by their parents, and it may have been twenty years, even longer. There's nothing they can do to change that. Once you have met Jesus Christ and made Him Lord of your life, you need to say, "Lord, I need You to help me forgive him for what he's done"—even to the point where you can walk up to that father who abused you, and say, "Because of Jesus Christ, I forgive you for what you've done to me."

If you can't get to that point, it will affect your marriage. It will affect your relationship with your children. It will affect you on the job. It will affect how you respond to people. Time is passing by, and you can't really enjoy life, because you can't get past what has happened.

When you have something that you cover up, and never talk about it to anyone, the devil has a hold on you, like a claw in your mind, a claw in your spirit. But when you uncover it, when you can trust someone—it could be your husband, your wife, a close Christian friend, a pastor—then the devil no longer has a tight grip.

When you are counseled by a man or woman of God, that Word makes a difference; if you don't have that to help you along, you can easily fall back into what you got out of.

For someone who has been abused, it's important to remember that maybe the parent who abused you was abused as a child too. You can be so involved in your own hurt, that you don't realize how bad the abuser might be hurting too. Recognizing that can help you begin the healing process of forgiveness.

One woman in our church pointed out, "If you're ever going to obey the Bible's command to honor your mother and father, you have to keep reminding yourself through all of this, 'It is still my mother; it's still my father.' That's the bottom line."

"It's not only the physical abuse; you have verbal abuse too," one woman in our church told me. "Parents need to be aware of what they tell their kids, because it can go on with them into their adult lives. Just recently, I was able to sit down with my mom to let her know what she said that stuck with me all this time, and how it affected my life."

She was able to do that on Easter Sunday, after hearing a sermon about forgiveness. Forgiveness is always the key. A lot of people are stuck in their past, because they don't know how to forgive. "He hurt me so bad, there's no way I can forgive him. I'm going to take this to my grave with me." So people take it to their graves with them.

What about when you have a major disagreement with your parents (after you're already living on your own)? How do you honor them? When I was ready to get out of the military, my father said, "Boy, you sure you heard from God, or the devil? You're going to be a full-time pastor. Son, I think you need to stay in the military. You have that paycheck coming."

"Dad, I heard what you said," I told him, "but I really believe that God told me to get out, so we're going to go ahead and do that. My wife is with me on that. I know I heard from God on this."

I still honored him in the sense that I wasn't disrespectful to him. That's what you need to do. Show them reverence. You can show them honor without obeying what they're saying. It's the spirit in which you do it.

Reflections

1. Communication is a key, not only to preserving and building relationship, but to restoring broken ones.

2. If we're always thinking about how we've been wronged, we're going to have a negative picture of our mate.

3. After you become a Christian, there is nothing a person can do to you that you shouldn't at least try to forgive.

4. No sin is beyond forgiveness, even murder.

5. A lot of people are stuck in the past because they don't know how to forgive.

Chapter 10

Making Marriage Work

What are some attitudes you need to have to make a marriage work? Here is a list I developed with the help of my congregation.

The word "divorce" should not be in the husband's or wife's vocabulary. To put that another way, divorce is not an option. If every couple had that attitude, we would have vastly fewer broken families, and vastly fewer people in poverty.

You need to recognize that marriage is something you have to work at. The work never stops.

Both individuals should have a strong commitment to making the marriage work.

Both of you have to have a heart of forgiveness.

Both of you need to realize that you are going to have some bad times. You should be ready for them, and expect them.

Both husband and wife need to have an attitude of cooperation. You need to recognize that you will have to deny yourselves in order to make the marriage work.

You need sensitivity to one another's needs.

You also should have an attitude that you won't allow little things to come between you.

You should be optimistic, but not have unrealistic expectations. You're not married to Superman or Wonderwoman.

Don't compare your spouse to your mother or father.

You should be making an effort to grow together. People change, and if you are trying to adapt yourself to your mate and trying to grow into the person God wants you to be, you will grow together, not grow apart.

Humility is essential. My definition of humility is this: when you realize that you don't know everything.

You need unconditional acceptance. Give and take. Realize that the opposite sex is different. Learn to come together and do what each other likes.

You should have an open line of communication with your spouse.

You must be able to trust one another.

Be committed to each other's best interest.

You should have mutual respect and admiration for each other's ideas and commitment.

You need to have the attitude that you belong to one another.

God's order is headship. None of us has the last word where our own lives are concerned. When we think about headship, we usually think about who's in charge of whom. But headship is not just about authority; it's about covering. Ephesians 5:23 tells us: *"The husband is the head of the wife as Christ is the head of the church, His body, of which He is the Savior."* Jesus Christ, the Bible tells us, is the ultimate authority (Eph. 1:20-21). He has authority over the Church; He is its head. We must obey Him—for our own good. This is a covering or protection.

We each need a covering. When we have someone to whom we submit, someone who can tell us, "No, I think you're wrong about that," it gives us protection. I have a covering. You have a covering. You can't just go from church to church. That is not scriptural at all.

Because people don't recognize what the Bible is teaching about authority, they can miss out on the blessings God has for them. In marriage, the man is God's appointed leader. This headship does not give him the right to act like a slavemaster, or to treat his wife like a servant. He is the head to protect her. A leader is supposed to be a servant first. The man is a servant to his wife.

Ephesians 5:25 tells husbands to love their wives just as Christ loved the Church and gave Himself up for her. A loving wife responds to a loving husband just like a loving Church responds to a loving Christ. A loving Church doesn't mind submitting to a loving Christ.

Ephesians 5:28 tells husbands to love their wives the way they love their own bodies. How do you love your body? You protect your body. You feed it. You clothe it. That's how husbands are to love their wives.

Ephesians 5:31 says that a man will leave his father and mother and be united to his wife.

First Peter 3:7 tells husbands to be considerate of their wives, and treat them with respect. Why would God have to tell us that? We overlook it.

Left to the human way of doing things, women's rights and opinions would be basically ignored by men. God wants us to treat them as the weaker vessels so that they will have rights, and so that women will not be lorded over by authoritarian men and be mistreated and abused.

The word "weak" in this case does not mean "lacking strength," because women are not weak. To have a baby, stay home and wash clothes, clean up a house and cook, and work—that takes strength, and not just physical endurance, but dedication, commitment, and perseverance. "Weak" in this case means "delicate." Women are more sensitive, and they have within them everything man needs to help him, to accent him, and to complement him.

Now, when something is delicate, you treat it special. Wives should be special, honored, privileged. Husbands must treat their wives with consideration. That means, for one thing, listening. A lot of men won't even consider what their wives have to say.

Some men put too much on their wives. They forget that they're women. A woman cannot go out and work a ten- or twelve-hour job and come home to do all the work at home too. That is not God's plan for women.

What does Ephesians say to wives? Ephesians 5:22-24 says, *"Wives, submit to your husbands as to the Lord."* Have the same loving attitude you have toward the Lord. Let submission be something you do willingly. *"For the husband is the head of the wife as Christ is the head of the church, His body, of which He is the Savior."* Wives are to recognize the headship of Christ in the headship of their husbands. *"Now as the church submits to Christ, so also wives should submit to their husbands in everything."* What if the woman is married to an unbeliever? It is very difficult to subject yourself to an unsaved person. It is almost an impossibility sometimes.

One woman in our church described submission this way: "It's taking my divine order." It involves accountability. In a sense, it means to honor, to reverence, the position of authority, of headship, ordered by God.

To the extent that the leadership of your husband is not asking you to do anything immoral, then in God's eyes the simple act of submission is good. If somebody told you to go outside and cut your fingers off, you would say, "No, I can't do that."

If an unsaved husband were to tell you, "Sit down and smoke some marijuana with me," you would have to say, "No, I can't do that." Sometimes there are flagrant, clear-cut things.

How do you know sometimes what you should do? We have the Holy Spirit in us. We are Christians, we love the Lord, we have the Holy Spirit. Some situations you might not have a right or wrong answer for, but there will be a check in your spirit about it. You may have to say, "Look, I just can't do that. I just can't do that. I'm sorry." You don't have to be defiant about it. God will give you guidance.

Reflections

1. The word "divorce" should not be in the husband's or wife's vocabulary.

2. You should have an open line of communication with your spouse.

3. In marriage, the man is God's appointed leader.

Chapter 11

Support and Forgiveness

The family is under attack, and the way to resist the attacks and to have victory over the enemy is to have unity in the husband-and-wife team. But that can seem impossible when one of the partners is a believing Christian and one is not.

Maybe you made the mistake of marrying someone who wasn't a Christian. Maybe you weren't a Christian yourself when you got married. Or maybe your spouse has wandered away from God. Maybe you have wandered away.

If you want to experience victory over the attacks of the enemy, you need to start building unity. I'm not saying that's easy. It means the cross, and that is never easy.

But it's our calling. God wants to see you and your whole household saved. And He promises that it can happen.

One of our Christian duties is to stand for the truth. Some of the things our president stands for are opposed to the Word of God. On a radio program, I heard a woman say, "I know that Clinton's platform is very, very ungodly, but we need to claim the Scripture 'All things work together for good.' "

That may be true. But it is up to us as Christians to let our light shine, so that we can blot out the darkness that's trying to cover this world. And any Christian who did not vote was really saying, "I don't care what happens." It is important that we stand up for what we believe in and for what the Word of God has to say.

Yes, God can bring good out of any situation, but that doesn't absolve us from our responsibility to oppose evil, to try to keep the bad situation from happening in the first place. The Kingdom of God is to be established in us, and whenever we submit to something ungodly, we are working against God. We cannot decline to vote and just say, "God's going to take care of it." When we have a spouse who is not a believing Christian, we cannot just say, "God's going to take care of it." That doesn't mean we fight with our spouse over religion. That won't do any good. It does mean we work to bring good out of the situation.

The Bible tells wives how to win unsaved husbands, and I think it also applies to husbands who want to win unsaved wives.

Regardless of whether that person is your husband or your wife, the Bible does not mean you submit to commands that require ungodly behavior of you. There's no way a godly woman will smoke marijuana with her husband. There is no way a godly woman would have sex with her husband's friend even if her husband asked her to. The Bible does say we are to submit. If it does not involve sin, we should die to self and give in. That way we will win the other person over. If your husband asks you to watch a football game with him and you hate football, watching the game with him will show him that you're more interested in pleasing him than in pleasing yourself. That's sacrificial love. If you're trying to get your husband to become a believer, then you're trying to get him to believe in sacrificial love. Show him some. The more you show him, the sooner he'll believe.

The Bible is all about sacrificial love. We need to show it in our lives. The Bible also condemns sin. But if we only live the parts about condemning sin, then the unbelieving spouse is going to be hearing nothing but condemnation. That's the opposite of what we're supposed to be teaching by example. In Christ there is no condemnation. Our spouses should see that in our lives.

First Peter 2:13 tells us: *"Submit yourselves for the Lord's sake to every authority instituted among men."* Not for your sake; for the Lord's sake.

Verses 16-18 say: *"...live as servants of God. Show proper respect to everyone...not only to those who are good and considerate, but also to those who are harsh."*

Sometimes at work you can find yourself in a situation where you have to put up with a lot and suffer for being a Christian. People will ostracize you and treat you different and want you to feel like you're nobody. But only the people who are different can make a difference in this world. Only those who stand above the crowd can really make a difference.

> *Wives...be submissive to your husbands, so that if any of them do not believe the Word, they may be won over without words by the behavior of their wives when they see the purity and reverence of your lives* (1 Pet. 3:1-2).

When I was a teenager, my father was in a car accident. A drunk hit him, and he was lying on top of the Savannah Bridge. His leg was broken in three places, and a little old lady came and put her pocketbook under his head. He lay there for hours. Then he spent a year on his back, with a cast from his neck to his toes. They said he'd never walk again. We had to take him back and forth to the bathroom, and it was terrible for him to be like that. We had to transport him all around the house. He just felt helpless.

One day, he was in the back bedroom sleeping. We had a wood-burning furnace, and the curtain caught on fire. We were all outside playing horseshoes. Finally we heard him screaming and we came in and took the curtain down. That night he said he didn't know how much longer he could take it. He called my mother in. "If you love me," he said, "I want you to go to Seven-Eleven and get me some ice cream."

"Dad," I said, "there's no way she's going to walk to Seven-Eleven at this time of night. I'll go get it."

"No," he said, "I want your mother to go."

"No," we said. "We're not letting our mother go out in the dark like this, no way."

"Boys," he said, "you all be quiet. I want your mom to go."

She was crying and she said, "I'll go, honey."

"If you love me," he said.

"I love you, honey."

It was an ego thing. But, you know, my mother was willing to walk to the store in the dark for him. We wanted to walk with her. "No, I want to go by myself," she said.

It was about a mile and a half, and it was dark. You couldn't see your hand in front of your face, it was so dark. She walked. I had a school bus, and I got into it. My brother got into his car, and we followed her and watched her the whole time.

Husbands may be won over without words by the behavior of their wives. The testing of the Word comes when you are put under pressure. Then, because of the love you have for the Lord, and for your husband, you submit.

Your husbands will be won over "*when they see the purity and reverence of your lives.*" That's what my father saw in my mother; that's what brought him to the Lord.

By submitting, by governing your behavior with reverence and purity, you develop inner strength. When I hear about some of the things women go through, I just don't know how they make it. Some men go through this stuff too, living with an unsaved wife. I don't see how they make it. It's just unbelievable. An inner beauty rather than an outward beauty is what carries them through. The unfailing beauty of a gentle and quiet spirit is of great worth in God's sight. Do what is right and do not give in to fear.

Let your love be real. "Sometimes a woman has a public face, a front," one woman in my church told me. "She submits to her husband in public, but at home she runs things. It shows that she doesn't have any respect for her husband."

This kind of marriage won't last; if it's not done the Bible way, it won't stand the pressure. Without the conviction of the Holy Spirit in my life, without the knowledge of the Word of God, without my desire to live for God, in our times of testing, we could have fallen too. Without God, I might be divorced right now.

Sometimes women show more respect for the pastor than for their own husbands. A saved man is really the pastor of his home. His wife is his co-pastor. When the wife doesn't have a pastor at home, she will often show more respect to the one who *is* pastoring her.

If the wife does not respect her husband, it is because of what she sees. Her husband is supposed to be her pastor in the home, and a pastor has to *live* the Word in order to have credibility, to have respect. If a pastor gets up in church and preaches a whole sermon about principles that he's not living himself, his wife won't be able to respect him, because she lives with him. She sees his life.

"It's hard for a woman to support a man she doesn't respect," one man in my church told me. "When a man doesn't have his wife's support, it's probably because she doesn't respect him as a person. If she doesn't respect him as a person, she can't respect the position that he's in."

When she supports her husband, she's telling him in a silent way that she respects him and believes in him, is going to support him, to back him. It is important for a man to know that his wife respects him.

When I was in the Air Force, there were times when I felt like quitting. One time when I had been in the service ten years, I was hoping to be an education services officer over in Europe. I wasn't sure that would work out, and I was thinking of getting out of the Air Force. My wife said, "Honey, you know, if you want to get out, if that's what you want to do, and you really feel good about it, I'll go with you. I don't want you to do anything that's going to make you lose your confidence in yourself. But would you just try to put in your paperwork for this officer program? And if that comes through, we'll go with that. If not, we'll get on out."

When you have that kind of support it increases your confidence. Even if you fall flat on your face, you know that you have someone to fall with you.

God wants the wife to respect her husband, to show that love. Even if you're husband is not a Christian, you can show him that kind of love and support. In fact, you're going to *have* to show him that kind of love and support if you want him to become a Christian. If you want him to believe in God's unconditional love, you've got to show him some of it.

If you're a husband whose wife is not a Christian, just love her, smother her with love. A woman has to be loved and shown love. Then her respect for you will be evident at home and outside the home.

I asked my congregation whether they thought it would be easier to live with an unsaved husband or an unsaved wife. One man answered, "Pastor, I think it would be just as hard to live with a lukewarm person." It probably would.

"Pastor," one woman said, "you get people who say they're saved but they don't want you to come to church. They act just like unsaved people. So basically, you don't know what you have. They come to church and say, 'I'm saved.' Then every time you get ready to go to church, or when you get ready to pay your tithe, or go to choir practice, you have a fight on your hands."

There is a time for Christians to fight: to fight evil, not to fight with each other or with our spouses. People believe in what they see. If we show anger and resentment to our mate, that makes it hard to believe in the divine love we're always talking about. If we want our spouses to believe in God's love, then we have to show them God's love in us.

Reflections

1. One of our Christian duties is to stand for the truth.

2. The Kingdom of God is to be established in us, and whenever we submit to something ungodly, we are working against God.

3. Only those who stand above the crowd can really make a difference.

4. If the wife does not respect her husband, it is because of what she sees.

5. It is important for a man to know that his wife respects him.

Chapter 12

Teaching the Children

"Honor your father and mother," we read in the Ten Commandments, which Moses brought down from Mount Sinai. This commandment, St. Paul tells us, is the first commandment with a promise.

Ephesians 6:1-4 says:

Children, obey your parents in the Lord, for this is right. "Honor your father and mother"—which is the first commandment with a promise—"that it may go well with you and that you may enjoy long life on the earth." Fathers, do not exasperate your children; instead, bring them up in the training and instruction of the Lord (Eph. 6:1-4).

We need to focus on the development of the next generation. A lot of times, we forget about the children. Our world is consuming them. A lot of children don't know who they are simply because the parents have failed. Often, they have failed to teach their children to give their own parents the honor and respect that is due. Instead, they merely exasperate their children. St. Paul gives this as the opposite of training and instruction in the Lord.

Fathers can provoke children. A father can say things to a child that will really wipe a child out. That's why fathers need to be very careful how they speak to their children.

Paul said that *fathers* are to bring the children up in the training and instruction of the Lord. A lot of people think that it's the job of mothers and women to bring the children to church and train them in the way of the Lord. That's not what the Word says. It is the father's responsibility.

You know that fathers are absent from many families, and mothers are so busy trying to take care of their families that many times they don't give the children what they really need. There are a lot of families with no love and no order.

Because so many fathers and mothers have neglected their duty, the family is getting weak. Families often lack the knowledge to train their children. Preachers nowadays have to concentrate on the development of the next generation; they can't count on the parents to pass on the faith. We have a responsibility to preach messages that will develop our young people. If we don't develop them, we're going to lose them.

As Vice President Dan Quayle pointed out, young people become gang members because they are looking for a family. They come from dysfunctional families that lack love and order. They join gangs looking for love, order and acceptance. Their families can't seem to give it to them, so they create their own families.

The time has come for us to strengthen our families. If we don't strengthen our families, we're going to lose the next generation. The family needs to be the classroom for the instruction of children. That means that the mother and the father are the primary teachers. In the family, children learn what they need to know. If the principal—the father—is not there, they've already lost. If the mother's not giving them what they need, they've lost. The mother and the father need to be the primary teachers.

Proverbs 1:7 tells us: *"The fear of the Lord is the beginning of knowledge, but fools despise wisdom and discipline."*

If you have a child who doesn't fear the Lord, both the child and you are fools. Verse 8 says: *"Listen, my son, to your father's instruction and do not forsake your mother's teaching."* Teachings are lessons. It's the responsibility of the mother to give the children lessons. Children used to regularly get spankings from their mothers, and spankings from their fathers now and then.

When I was in sixth grade, living in Philadelphia, I went and told my mother the biggest lie. I told her I had to have a blue suit with some white shoes. Now, when I was in sixth grade, white shoes and a blue suit were the thing. She wanted her son to have what everybody else had, so she went out and bought me a blue suit and white shoes. So I got my blue suit and white shoes and went to sixth-grade graduation, and I was the only boy there with a blue suit and white shoes. I was cool. Everybody else had on a white shirt and blue pants.

But I wasn't cool when I got home. My mother gave me a spanking that I never forgot. All I remember was saying, "I'm not going to do it again."

My mother disciplined me. She's the one I lied to, she's the one who was primarily hurt by the lie, and she's the one who gave me the spanking.

The Bible says that when a child is unruly, it primarily reflects on the mother and the lessons she is teaching the children. Proverbs 29:15 says, "*The rod of correction imparts wisdom, but a child left to himself disgraces his mother.*"

A mother's love is something else. You can turn on the television and see a serial killer who has murdered twenty or thirty people, and his mother will come on and say, "That's my child. He's really a good boy." A mother's love should be unconditional, but it's also her responsibility to teach those lessons.

But people are forgetting about the children. They're getting divorces right and left, because all they're thinking about is themselves. They're forgetting the children.

It seem to be getting harder for marriages to stay together. People, it seems, just can't get along. They don't want to be married anymore. So many marriages are wearing themselves out, and they're not being revitalized. They get married again and raise another family. If that doesn't work, they get married again and raise *another* family.

Then we have gangs taking over our nation because the children are going to revolt over what we're doing to them.

Your marriage is the thing that makes the family. We've got to make our marriages last. We've got to learn how to hang in there. We've got to learn how to never quit. We've got to learn how to say, "I'm going to get up again, and try again." We owe it to the next generation. We owe it to our children.

Every married man and woman is responsible for what becomes of his/her home. It isn't up to the children. You can't excuse yourself by saying, "I was a victim of circumstance." There's a reason why children are running around in the streets shooting people: they had a mother and father who were not mother and father to them. The parents are causing the problem.

My children are an extension of me. If you have unruly children, they are an extension of you. You can't blame it on anyone else. If you have a lot of fighting in your home, a lot of tension and stress, your children will show it. Husbands and wives, fathers and mothers, are the primary teachers.

But what are we teaching the children? They are learning about marriage and family life by watching how we live.

They see women and men making mistakes that are wearing out their marriages:

Women act like mothers and treat their men like children. That's what's destroying some of our men. Men, stand up and be a man! Say, "Don't talk to me like that! I'm not your child."

Women, you need to make a list of how you make your husband feel like a child. Just say, "I'm going to stop doing that. I'm going to stop trying to make him feel like a child."

A second mistake is that women take charge of things because they feel that the man can't do it right. If he messes it up all the time, let him mess it up and make a fool of himself. Let him come to you for help. But don't just move in and take over.

Another mistake is one that men make: men are emotionally out of shape. They're not caring enough. Men are not sensitive enough to women. They don't know how to be sensitive or caring. Men don't know how to express themselves. They need to open up. They want to keep everything inside, and they take it out on their wives by just not being responsive to their needs.

The second mistake men make is to hold women back from becoming all they can be. Men, you need to stop getting intimidated by women who want to be all they can be.

Here's a word for single women who are thinking about marrying: Always look for a man who wants you to shine. If a man wants to hold you down or hold you back, there will always be some problems communicating.

There is a very close link between love and understanding. A lot of married couples have problems because they feel that they have gotten to the place where they understand each other. That's a very dangerous place to be. Women are very complicated and men are very complicated. We're very, very different. One of the first things we have to understand is that we are different. We have to recognize and accept the difference. Women see things differently and men see things differently.

We need to recognize the differences but try to understand. There is a close link between love and understanding. When you think you have understood your mate, you're in trouble, because we keep changing. We're so different that we never completely understand. But we've got to keep trying.

Why are men the way they are? Why are women the way they are? Because God made them the way they are.

One thing women need to understand about men: men hate to be wrong. They hate to be told that they are wrong. And a man hates it when a woman knows he is wrong and tells him.

Women say things like "Why don't you stop and ask for directions?" What the man hears is "You're stupid."

You said it real nice: "Why don't you ask for directions?" You don't see anything wrong with it. But the man never likes to be told he's wrong.

I went to South Carolina, to my home town, a couple of years ago. I just flew down there by myself to be with my mother and father. We were riding along in the car. My father wanted to show me some places he'd been in his job. "Son," he said, "all over here, it's all built up now, all hotels all over here." Then he said, "Let me take this highway here." Men like to be in charge, too.

My mother said, "It's not that highway. That's the wrong highway."

"Look, I've been traveling these roads for twenty years!" Then he kept telling me, "Ah, son, all this has been developed."

"Well, Dad," I said, "this is pretty good."

My mother said, "You took the wrong highway."

"Dear, I travel these roads all the time." About twenty minutes later, when we were getting ready to go back home, my father couldn't seem to find his way back. He looked at my mother and said, "Dear, could you tell me how to get out of here?"

Another time, my mother and father went to a banquet, and he was supposed to be in charge. They went in and greeted everybody, and were talking and laughing, and my mother kept saying, "Daddy..."

"What is it, Dear?" he responded, without really paying attention. My father shook everybody's hand, and ended up at the head table. Somebody invited him to be at the head table. When it was time for dinner to be served, he looked around, and said, "I don't know any of these people in here."

"I was trying to tell you," my mother said, "you came to the wrong banquet."

"Just don't make me look like a fool," my father said. "Let's just stay like we know what we're doing."

Sometimes men rush in and mess things up, but wait till they come to you for help. Don't rush in yourself to take over.

These may seem like little things, but they are part of Kingdom living—giving in, being considerate, putting yourself last, putting the other person first.

Jesus should be the most important person in our life. But within the family, who's the most important person? It should be your husband or your wife. When the children can see that the husband and the wife get along, you can relate that love and order to the children. And we need to have the attitude that whatever it takes to make our marriage last, that's what we'll do, because we have to think about the next generation, the children. We're teaching and forming them right now by the way we live.

Reflections

1. The time has come for us to strengthen our families.

2. If we don't strengthen our families, we're going to lose the next generation.

3. Every married man and woman is responsible for what becomes of his or her home.

Available from Dr. LaSalle R. Vaughn

Sex Is a Gift Not a Goal
by Dr. LaSalle R. Vaughn

$10.00 donation

Workbooks are also available

Teaching Tapes by Dr. LaSalle Vaughn

Tape	Donation
How to Know the Voice of God	$14.95
Motivation	$19.95
Seven Sins of the Wicked	$14.95
God's Perfect Timing	$14.95
The Family	$39.95
Church Conflict	$15.95
Spiritual Dynamics of Relationships	$15.95
Authority	$16.95
Developing a Godly Self-Image	$15.95
The Prime of '92 (The 12 best sellers of 1992)	$24.95
Why Men & Women Need Each Other	$19.95

Qty	Product	Donation	Total
	Shipping and Handling		
	Total		

Guarantee: You may return any defective item within 90 days for replacement. Please allow 4 weeks for delivery.

Make Checks Payable to: New Life Ministries

Send orders to:

New Life Ministries
6610 Hwy. 90 West
San Antonio, TX 78227
(210) 679-6050